DOCUMENTS
of the
INDUSTRIAL
REVOLUTION
1750–1850

DOCUMENTS
of the
INDUSTRIAL
REVOLUTION
1750–1850

Edited by
RICHARD L. TAMES

HUTCHINSON EDUCATIONAL

HUTCHINSON EDUCATIONAL LTD

178–202 Great Portland Street, London W1

London Melbourne Sydney
Auckland Johannesburg Cape Town
and agencies throughout the world

First published 1971

*This book has been set in Fournier type, printed in Great Britain
on smooth wove paper by Anchor Press, and
bound by Wm. Brendon, both of Tiptree, Essex*

ISBN 0 09 106650 6 (cased)
0 09 106651 4 (paper)

Contents

Documents

xiv

Acknowledgements

The author and publishers are very grateful to the following for permission to reproduce source material:

Allen and Unwin Ltd for extracts from *Human Documents of the Victorian Golden Age*, by E. Royston Pike, and *A History of Western Technology*, by F. Klemm;

E. J. Arnold and Son Ltd for extracts from *Land, Labour and Population in the Industrial Revolution*, by Jones and Mingay, *Engineers, Inventors and Workers*, by P. W. Kingsford, *Essays in Economic History, Volume 3*, by Carus-Wilson, and *The Genesis of Modern Management*, by S. Pollard;

B. T. Batsford Ltd for extracts from *James Watt* by L. T. C. Rolt, and *Tools for the Job*, by L. T. C. Rolt;

G. Bell and Sons Ltd for extracts from *English Economic History* by Bland, Brown and Tawney;

Basil Blackwell and Mott Ltd for extracts from *How They Lived 1700-1815*, by Asa Briggs;

Cambridge University Press for extracts from *The Cambridge Economic History of Europe, Vol VI*, by D. S. Landes;

Jonathan Cape Ltd for extracts from *Industrial Revolution in the Eighteenth Century*, by P. Mantowe;

Frank Cass & Co Ltd for extracts from *Development of Transportation in Modern England*, by Jackman, *History of the English Corn Laws*, by D. G. Barnes, *A History of Factory Legislation*, by Hutchins and Harrison;

English Universities Press Ltd for extracts from *Science and Technology in the Industrial Revolution*, by A. E. Musson and E. Robinson;

Eyre & Spottiswoode (Publishers) Ltd for extracts from *English Historical Documents*;

Faber & Faber Ltd for extracts from *A Social History of Engineering*, by W. H. G. Armytage;

Victor Gollancz Ltd for extracts from *The Making of the English Working Class*, by E. P. Thompson;

Longman Group Limited for extracts from *England's Apprenticeship 1603-1763*, by Charles Wilson, *The Annual Register, Vol 56*, and *The Town Labourer*, by J. L. and B. Hammond;

Macmillan & Co Ltd for extracts from *Readings in Economic and Social History*, by M. W. Flinn, and *Working Class Movements* by Cole and Filson;

Manchester University Press for extracts from *A History of Macclesfield*, by C. S. Davies, and *A History of Shops and Shopping*, by C. S. Davies;

Odham Books for extracts from *Victorian Cities*, by Asa Briggs;

Penguin Books Ltd for extracts from *A Documentary History of England (1559-1931)*, by E. M. Williams, *England in Transition*, by M. D. George, *London Life in the 18th Century*, by M. D. George, and *The Common Muse*, by V. de Sola Pinto and A. E. Rodway.

Introduction

As Professor Asa Briggs has written, 'however precise the statistics, something more than accuracy and discipline are needed in the study of social and economic history. ... Behind the abstractions of economist or sociologist is the experience of real people, who demand sympathetic understanding as well as searching analysis. One of the dangers of economic history is that it can be written far too easily in impersonal terms: real people seem to play little part in it.' This warning note provided the starting point for the following selection of documents, which consists almost entirely of extracts from letters, diaries, pamphlets and official publications. Statistics and statutes are absent from the selection as the intention has been to complement the source publications which already exist. Inevitably there have been omissions, most notably finance and banking, but it is hoped that the documents presented will be helpful and stimulating to the majority of students for whom this work is intended.

Part 1

THE
EXPANDING
ECONOMY

The Process of Economic Growth

A general view of England, 1724

Even before industrialisation Britain enjoyed a level of prosperity which put her second only to Holland in terms of income per head. Woollen cloth was the chief export and single largest manufacturing industry; as such it provided skills and enterprise on which the later cotton industry could build. The surplus of grain produced in the first half of the eighteenth century on the one hand gave rise to an epidemic of gin drinking which threatened the health and morals of the nation, on the other created a 'slack' of agricultural capacity which was taken up later in the century to support the sudden and rapid upsurge in population which began around the middle years of the century. Britain's mineral wealth was, of course, the basis of the heavy industry sector which led the advance of industrialisation and provided the fuel, machinery and constructional materials for the rest of the economy.

DOCUMENT I

Herman Moll, A New Description of England and Wales
Quoted in English Historical Documents, Vol. X

The soil here is so very fruitful, especially in Corn, that the Island was anciently call'd the Granary of the Western World; and we cannot but think that it may still in a great Degree deserve that Name, because at present some of the greatest Kingdoms in *Europe* are supply'd with that necessary Support of Life from hence. In a Word, *England*, which no other Nation can with so much Justice pretend to, produces of itself all that can really conduce either to the Necessities and Convenience, or to the Pleasures and Satisfaction of Life; most of her Plenties and Ornaments being expressed in this old Verse.

> Anglis, 1 Mons, 2 Pons, 3 Fons, 4 Ecclesia,
> 5 Foemina, 6 Lana.
> For Mountains, Bridges, Rivers, Churches fair,
> Women and Wool, *England's* past compare.

There is no need of descanting upon these Particulars, nor on the rich Treasures the Bowels of the Earth afford us, in greater Plenty and Variety than to any of our neighbouring Nations; such Lead, Tin, Copper, Coals, etc. . . .

A Mass Market

England's relative prosperity, relative to the rest of Europe that is, gave entrepreneurs a market for consumer goods, like cloth, hardware, and pottery, a market which was, moreover, expanding and less liable to sudden and violent fluctuations, as export markets were. This atmosphere of well-being (the income per head in eighteenth-century England has been reckoned as twice as high as twentieth-century Nigeria or India) encouraged entrepreneurs to launch new products and invest in new processes of production.

DOCUMENT 2

D. Defoe, A Plan of the English Commerce (1728), pp 76–7
Quoted by D. S. Landes in The Cambridge Economic History of Europe, Vol VI, Part I, p 281

. . . for the rest, we see their Houses and Lodgings tolerably furnished, at least stuff'd well with useful and necessary household Goods: Even those we call poor People, Journey-men, working and pains-taking People do thus: they lye warm, live in Plenty, work hard and know no Want.

These are the People that carry off the Gross of your Consumption; 'tis for these your Markets are kept open late on *Saturday* nights: because they usually receive their Week's Wages late. . . . in a Word, these are the Life of our whole Commerce, and all by their Multitude: Their Numbers are not Hundreds or Thousands, or Hundreds of Thousands, but Millions; 'tis by their Multitude, I say, that all the Wheels of Trade are set on Foot, the Manufacture and Produce of the Land and Sea, finish'd, cur'd, and fitted for the Markets Abroad; 'tis by the Largeness of their Gettings, that they are supported, and by the Largeness of their Number the whole Country is supported; by their Wages they are able to live plentifully, and it is by their expensive, generous, free way of living, that the Home Consumption is rais'd to such a Bulk, as well of our own, as of foreign Production. . . .

Progress of Rationalism

One of the more notable features of English social and political

4

life in the eighteenth century was the reality of religious scepti-
cism and the limited power of the constitutional monarchy,
sources of wonder to foreign visitors, whether they saw these
features as enlightened or deplorable. Britain was fortunate in
having no great established Church, with associated monasteries,
to suck up wealth and talent, and no magnificent court to crush
the industrious with taxation or interfere with the day-to-day
conduct of commerce in the interests of the king or his courtiers.
Men of enterprise were therefore relatively free to pursue their
own material advantage without fear of offending Heaven or
its earthly representatives. Gunnar Myrdal in his *Asian Drama*
has recently stressed the importance of values and attitudes in
promoting economic growth by the willing exploitation of
natural and human resources for limited and worldly ends.

DOCUMENT 3

Hume Essays (1741), I, vii

There has been a sudden and sensible change in the opinions of men within
these last fifty years, by the progress of learning and of liberty. Most people,
in this island, have divested themselves of all superstitious reverence to
names and authority. The clergy have entirely lost their credit: Their pre-
tensions and doctrines have been ridiculed; and even religion can scarcely
support itself in the world. The name of king commands little respect, and
to talk of a king as God's viceregent on earth, or to give him any of those
magnificent titles which formerly dazzled mankind, would but excite
laughter.

Production For Modest Incomes

It is perhaps misleading to talk of income per head, which is an
economist's calculation rather than a social reality. The 'mass
market', in so far as it existed in eighteenth-century England,
consisted of a substantial group of farmers, skilled craftsmen,
innkeepers and public functionaries, rather than the masses of
the labouring poor who had but a few pence to spare above bare
subsistence, and that chiefly to be spent on ale or trifling
novelties.

Dean Tucker, Instructions for Travellers (1758)
Quoted in Asa Briggs, How They Lived 1700–1815, p. 150

Q. Are the Men of England, those especially in the Toy, Jewellery, Cabinet, Furniture and Silk Trades chiefly adapted for high or middling life and what Species of People make up the Bulk of the Customers?
A. England, being a free Country, where Riches got by Trade are no Disgrace, and where Property is also safe . . . and where every Person may make what Display he pleases of his wealth . . . the Manufacturers of the Kingdom accommodate themselves, if I may so speak, to the Constitution of it: That is that they are more adapted to the Demands of Peasants and Mechanics . . . for Farmers, Freeholders, Tradesmen and Manufacturers in middling Life and for Wholesale Dealers, Merchants, and all Persons of Landed Estates, to appear in genteel Life; than for the Magnificence of Palaces, or the Cabinets of Princes. Thus that is, according to the very Spirit of our Constitution, that the English of these several Denominations have better Conveniences in their Houses, and appear to have more in Quantity of clean neat Furniture, and a greater Variety (such as Carpets, Screens, Window Curtains . . . Bells polished Brass Locks, Fenders etc. Things hardly known among Persons abroad of such a Rank) than in any other Country in Europe, Holland excepted.

Importance of Fashion

The relative 'openness' of eighteenth-century society gave the ambitious the hope of rising in society. Arkwright started life as a barber and ended as a knight and High Sheriff of his county, with a fortune of half a million pounds. On their way up these nouveaux riches acquired a status consciousness which was imitated by those with similar aspirations. The very fluidity of the social structure found expression in patterns of expenditure and behaviour. Commentators were appalled that servants could be indistinguishable from solid citizens in their new cotton clothes and Wedgwood made his fortune by making the tableware of the elegant and the successful available in quantity to their admirers. He sold the people what they thought they ought to want.

*T. Forster, An Enquiry into the Causes of the Present High Price of
Provisions (1767), p 41*
*Quoted in E. W. Gilboy, 'Demand as a Factor in the Industrial Revolution',
in The Causes of the Industrial Revolution (ed. R. M. Hartwell)*

In England the several ranks of men slide into each other almost impercep-
tibly; and a spirit of equality runs through every part of the constitition.
Hence arises a strong emulation in all the several stations and conditions to
vie with each other; and a perpetual restless ambition in each of the inferior
ranks to raise themselves to the level of those immediately above them. In
such a state as this fashion must have an uncontrolled sway. And a fashionable luxury must spread though it like a contagion.

The basis of economic progress is increasing occupational
specialisation. Adam Smith's influential example of the pin
factory is the classic statement of this dictum.

DOCUMENT 6

*Adam Smith, Inquiry into the Nature and Causes of the Wealth of Nations
(1776), Vol I, Ch I, pp 6–7*

A workman not educated to this business (which the division of labour has
rendered a distinct trade), nor acquainted with the use of the machinery
employed in it (to the invention of which the same division of labour has
probably given occasion), should scarce, perhaps, with his utmost industry,
make one pin in a day, and certainly could not make twenty. But in the way
in which this business is now carried on, not only the whole work is a peculiar trade, but it is divided into a number of branches, of which the greater
part are likewise peculiar trades. One man draws out the wire; another
straights it; a third cuts it; a fourth points it; a fifth grinds it at the top for
receiving the head; to make the head requires two or three distinct operations; to put it on is a peciliar business; to whiten the pin is another; it is
even a trade by itself to put them into the paper; and the important business
of making a pin is in this manner divided into about eighteen distinct
operations, which, in some manufactories, are all performed by distinct
hands, though in others the same man will sometimes perform two or three
of them. I have seen a small manufactory of this kind, where ten men only
were employed, and where some of them, consequently, performed two
or three distinct operations. But though they were very poor, and, therefore,
but indifferently accommodated with the necessary machinery, they could,
when they exerted themselves, make among them about twelve pounds of
pins a day. There are in a pound upwards of four thousand pins of a middling

size. Ten persons, therefore, could make among them upwards of forty-eight thousand pins in a day . . .

The Importance of Enterprises

Arthur Young, who wrote chiefly on agriculture, travelled extensively on the continent, as well as in England. Like many of his contemporaries he emphasised the value of individual thought and enterprise. It is important to remember that eighteenth-century England had the social and intellectual climate to welcome rather than stifle new ideas. As Dr. Johnson remarked with some disapproval: 'The age is running mad after innovation; all the business of the world is to be done in a new way; men are to be hanged in a new way; Tyburn itself is not safe from the fury of innovation.'

DOCUMENT 7

Arthur Young, Tours in England & Wales, p 269

Get rid of that dronish, sleepy, and stupid indifference, that lazy negligence, which enchains men in the exact paths of their forefathers, without enquiry, without thought, and without ambition, and you are sure of doing good. What trains of thought, what a spirit of exertion, what a mass and power of effort have sprung in every path of life from the works of such men as Brindley, Watt, Priestley? Harrison, Arkwright . . . ?

Population Growth

The extent of the rapid rise in population between 1750 and 1850 is not questioned, but the causes are a matter of controversy and contemporary opinions on this highly technical and complex subject are suspect. The theory that medical advances were responsible has been discredited but no simple theory has been put in its place. For a recent summary of the situation see M. W. Flinn's pamphlet 'British Population Growth 1700–1850' (Macmillan). It is a matter for debate whether rising population prompted the expansion of economic activity or whether the expansion of economic activity called forth a new labour force, or whether both processes took place simultaneously.

A. Young, North of England, Vol IV, p 411

It is employment that creates population. There is not an instance in the whole globe of an idle people being numerous in proportion to their territory, but, on the contrary, all industrious countries are populous, and proportionable to the degree of their industry. When employment is plentiful and time of value, families are not burdens, marriages are early and numerous. . . . It is an absolute impossibility that, in such circumstances, the people should not increase. . . .

Importance of High Wages

Adam Smith's generalisation about wage levels is, perhaps, rather too crude to be of much use as an analytical concept but it does represent a considerable contrast to the opinions current in the earlier part of the century that only poverty kept the labouring classes industrious. Both assertions have a measure of truth. High wages could mean thrift, diligence and self-improvement, but only when they came in regularly. Wages which were only high for a few weeks at a time were too transient a feature of a worker's life to alter his pattern of behaviour; such temporary prosperity was dissipated in increased leisure or increased alcohol.

DOCUMENT 9

Adam Smith, Wealth of Nations (1776), Vol I, p 91

The liberal reward of labour, as it encourages the propagation, so it increases the industry of the common people. . . . A plentiful subsistence increases the bodily strength of the labourer, and the comfortable hope of bettering his condition, and of ending his days perhaps in ease and plenty, animates him to exert that strength to the utmost. Where wages are high, accordingly, we shall always find the workmen more active, diligent, and expeditious, than where they are low. . . .

Cheap Fuel and Improved Machinery

This perceptive summary of Britain's economic strengths (falling production costs, increasingly capital-intensive industry, and an improved system of internal transport) gives the historian a useful, if incomplete 'model' of the process of economic growth.

Note that the 'interruptions of commerce with America' became far more serious when actual war broke out in 1776.

DOCUMENT 10

*M.S. Letter, 28th September 1775. PRO Colonial Office, 5/154 no. 188
Quoted in M. D. George, England in Transition, pp 110-11*

From the observations I have made of the state of the manufactories in general, I am induced to think that the present flourishing condition is not a little owing to the two following causes, viz.: first, the great improvements in Machinery, by which the expense of labour is much diminished and the perfection of the work increased; secondly, the cheapness of fuel, which is more universally diffused by means of internal navigation and the more easy communication by land, to which may be added the universal practice of cultivating potatoes which are experimentally found to be the cheapest of all food. These causes make the manufacturers to sell their commodities at a cheaper rate, while at the same time the degree of perfection [to] which their several branches are now brought, open to them a ready market in most parts of Europe; an advantage to this country which I apprehend will continue to increase; for although the wages of manufacturers in foreign countries are lower than here, yet the benefit arising from the large stock employed in trade in England, with the great improvement in machinery, and the plenty of fuel so absolutely necessary in most of the manufactories, do much more than counter-balance that circumstance. To this great consumption of our commodities on the Continent, I presume it is owing that the interruptions of commerce with America has been little felt.

Small-Scale Enterprise

The small scale of capital required to start up in business was one of the crucial factors in Britain's industrialisation. In cotton, the first industry to adopt mechanised production wholeheartedly, production could be started on rented spinning machines in the corner of a rented building, working on materials obtained on credit from a dealer. Weaving was largely performed by hand-workers labouring at their own looms in their own homes. The capital required in such a situation could easily be raised by a man of enterprise and determination, either from his own savings or from those of his relatives or friends. If the market were prosperous debts were repaid and the remaining profits 'ploughed back' into the business, which generated the capital for its own development. Slender capital reserves also meant waves of bankruptcies when markets collapsed but there were always new men waiting to push forward and take the places thus unwillingly vacated.

DOCUMENT 11

B. Foujas de Saint-Fond, Travels in England, Scotland and the Hebrides (1799), p 136
Quoted in S. Pollard, The Genesis of Modern Management

This modest simplicity (wrote Saint-Fond on the occasion of a visit to a Newcastle glassworks in 1784) is of great advantage to the country; it encourages active and industrious men to embark in trade, who would otherwise be unwilling to form large establishments, being alarmed by the expenses which extensive works require, when constructed on a magnificent scale. It is a taste for pomp and grandeur which almost always ruins the manufactures of France, and prevents those new ones which we want from being established: men are afraid to involve themselves in ruinous expenses for mere warehouses and workshops.

The Displacement of Agriculture

At the end of the eighteenth century agriculture was still the biggest single 'industry', employing about a third of the labour force and contributing about the same proportion to the National Income, but increasingly certain areas were taking on the aspect of extended industrial districts—the West Midlands, South-East Lancashire, the West Riding most noticeably of all.

DOCUMENT 12

W. Pitt, General View of the Agriculture of the county of Stafford (1794), pp 159–65
Quoted in English Historical Documents, Vol XI, p 521

The manufactures of Staffordshire are very considerable, and comprehend a variety of articles, particularly hardware, nails, toys, japanned goods, and potter's ware; also productions in cotton, silk, leather, woollen, linen, and many other articles.

Of the population of Staffordshire, I suppose one-third are supported by agricultural or other professions or employments thereon depending, and two-thirds by manufactures, commerce and mines. . . .

The following extract again emphasises the importance of individual enterprise and the application of machinery. Notice the reference to 'market research' and the implication of responsiveness to changes in the nature of demand; it is interesting that these comments should refer to the woollen industry, which was rather slow in adopting machinery, and which lost its primacy in exports about the time that this Report was written.

DOCUMENT 13

Report from the Committee on the state of the woollen manufacture of England (1806)
Quoted in English Historical Documents, Vol XI

. . . The rapid and prodigious increase of late years in the manufactures and commerce of this country is universally known, as well as the effects of that increase on our revenue and national strength; and in considering the immediate causes of that augmentation, it will appear that, under the favour of Providence, it is principally to be ascribed to the general spirit of enterprise and industry among a free and enlightened people, left to the unrestrained exercise of their talents in the employment of a vast capital; pushing to the utmost the principle of the division of labour; calling in all the resources of scientific research and mechanical ingenuity; and, finally, availing themselves of all the benefits to be derived from visiting foreign countries, not only for forming new, and confirming old commercial connections, but for obtaining a personal knowledge of the wants, the tastes, the habits, the discoveries and improvements, the productions and fabrics of other civilised nations, and, by thus bringing home facts and suggestions, perfecting our existing manufactures, and adding new ones to our domestic stock; opening at the same time new markets for the product of our manufacturing and commercial industry, and qualifying ourselves for supplying them. It is by these means alone, and, above all, your committee must repeat it, by the effect of machinery in improving the quality and cheapening the fabrication of our various articles of export, that with a continually accumulating weight of taxes, and with all the necessaries and comforts of life gradually increasing in price, the effects of which on the wages of labour, could not but be very considerable, our commerce and manufactures have been also increasing in such a degree as to surpass the most sanguine calculations of the ablest political writers who had speculated on the improvements of a future age. . . .

The wars against revolutionary and Napoleonic France lasted from 1793 to 1815 and necessitated an expenditure of £1,000,000,000. The effects of the war on industry were complex. Half a million men were drawn from the labour market to serve on land and sea; this certainly created bottlenecks in production and local scarcities of labour, which stimulated the adoption of labour-saving machinery. The demands of both agriculture and the services for horses raised their price; bad harvests raised the price of feed; these factors may have induced mine-owners to take to steam-power, where formerly a horse-gin had satisfied them. The award of government contracts for guns, uniforms and ships favoured those larger enterprises which were most likely to introduce the newest production techniques in their attempts to keep up with the extraordinary demands of war. The Navy led the way here, with the first set of steam-powered machinery designed to replace skilled labour for an entire process. The block-making machinery installed in Portsmouth dockyard in 1803 at a cost of £50,000 was designed by Marc Isambard Brunel and substituted the labour of over 100 craftsmen by the efforts of ten unskilled labourers.

DOCUMENT 14

Robert Owen, Report to the Committee of the Association for the Relief of the Manufacturing Poor, March 1817
Quoted in Cole and Filson, British Working Class Movements, Selected Documents 1789–1875

The introduction of mechanism into the manufacture of objects of desire in society reduced their price; the reduction of price increased the demand for them, and generally to so great an extent as to occasion more human labour to be employed after the introduction of machinery than had been employed before.

The first effects of these new mechanical combinations were to increase individual wealth, and to give a new stimulus to further inventions.

Thus one mechanical improvement gave rise to another in rapid succession; and in a few years they were not only generally introduced into the manufactures of these kingdoms, but were eagerly adopted by other nations of Europe, and by America.

Individual wealth soon advanced to national prosperity, as that term is generally understood; and the country, during a war of twenty-five years, demanding exertion and an amount of expenditure unknown at any former period, attained to a height of political power which confounded its foes and astonished its friends.

. . . But peace at length followed, and found Great Britain in possession of a new power in constant action, which, it may be safely stated, exceeded the labour of *one hundred millions* of the most industrious human beings, in the full strength of manhood.

. . . Thus our country possessed, at the conclusion of the war, a productive power, which operated to the same effect as if her population had been actually increased fifteen or twentyfold; and this had been chiefly created within the preceding twenty-five years.

Laissez-Faire

Individualism and Laissez-faire

Adam Smith's *Wealth of Nations* published in 1776 claimed to be an enquiry into the factors which made some nations wealthier than others. More than merely observing and recording, Smith was concerned to prescribe and recommend. His economic principles and indeed the *Wealth of Nations* itself, were part of a much larger theory of human behaviour which he eventually hoped to extend to cover all aspects of social and individual activity. At the root of Smith's theories lay the assumption that man is by nature a rational being, seeking always to maximise his material welfare and calculating the means by which he is to advance his personal self-interest.

DOCUMENT 15

Adam Smith, Wealth of Nations (1776), Vol I, pp 398–400

Every individual is continually exerting himself to find out the most advantageous employment for whatever capital he can command. It is his own advantage, indeed, and not that of the society, which he has in view. But the study of his own advantage naturally, or rather necessarily, leads him to prefer that employment which is most advantageous to the society.

... As every individual, therefore, endeavours as much as he can both to employ his capital in the support of domestic industry and so to direct that industry that its produce may be of the greatest value, every individual necessarily labours to render the annual revenue of the society as great as he can. He generally indeed, neither intends to promote the public interest nor knows how much he is promoting it. By preferring the support of domestic to that of foreign industry, he intends only his own security; and by directing that industry in such a manner as its produce may be of the greatest value, he intends only his own gain, and he is in this, as in many other cases, led by an invisible hand to promote an end which was no part of his intention. Nor is it always the worse for the society that it was no part of it. By pursuing his own interest he frequently promotes that of the society more effectually than when he really intends to promote it. I have never known much good done by those who affected to trade for the public good. It is an affectation, indeed, not very common among merchants, and very few words need to be employed in dissuading them from it.

The Ineptitude of Governments

Since the medieval period governments had sought to strengthen and control the means by which the wealth of nations has been produced. The notion of economic growth as such was absent, but the notion of promoting industries which were of general or strategic importance recommended itself to nearly every European nation. In the interests of social and economic stability wages, prices, conditions of work and even the processes of production themselves, were subject to extensive regulations. In eighteenth-century England these controls were increasingly ignored or evaded. Adam Smith provided a rationale for the prescriptions of economic advantage.

DOCUMENT 16

Adam Smith, Wealth of Nations, Vol I, pp 309–10

Though the profusion of government must, undoubtedly, have retarded the natural progress of England towards wealth and improvement, it has not been able to stop it. The annual produce of its land and labour is, undoubtedly, much greater at present than it was either at the restoration or at the revolution. The capital, therefore, annually employed in cultivating this land, and in maintaining this labour, must likewise be much greater. In the midst of all the exactions of government, this capital has been silently and gradually accumulated by the private frugality amd good conduct of individuals, by their universal, continual, and uninterrupted effort to better their own condition. It is this effect, protected by law and allowed by liberty to exert itself in the manner that is most advantageous, which has maintained the progress of England towards opulence and improvement in almost all former times. England, however, as it has never been blessed with a very parsimonious government, so parsimony has at no time been the characterised virtue of its inhabitants. It is the highest impertinence and presumption, therefore, in kings and ministers, to pretend to watch over the economy of private people, and to restrain their expense, either by sumptuary laws, or by prohibiting the importation of foreign luxuries. They are themselves always, and without any exception, the greatest spendthrifts in the society. Let them look well after their own expense, and they may safely trust private people with theirs. If their own extravagance does not ruin the state, that of their subjects never will.

The True Tasks of Government

Governments, in Adam Smith's ideal words, were to perform only those tasks which the self-interest of the individual did not recommend him to perform, but which remained needful for society as a whole. Smith specifically exempted the restrictive Navigation Acts from his general disapproval of government orders and prohibitions. The Navigation Acts, which originated in Britain's contest for maritime supremacy against Holland in the seventeenth century and which required that British trade should be carried on in British ships (thus creating a mercantile reserve which could be mobilised in time of war), were permissible, for defence had to come before opulence.

DOCUMENT 17

Adam Smith, Wealth of Nations, Vol II, pp 180–1

It is thus that every system which endeavours, either by extraordinary encouragements to draw towards a particular species of industry a greater share of the capital of the society than would naturally go to it, or, by extraordinary restraints, force from a particular species of industry some share of the capital which would otherwise be employed in it, is in reality subversive to the great purpose which it means to promote. It retards, instead of accelerating, the progress of the society towards real wealth and greatness; and diminishes, instead of increasing, the real value of the annual produce of its land and labour.

All systems either of preference or of restraint, therefore, being thus completely taken away, the obvious and simple system of natural liberty establishes itself of its own accord. Every man, as long as he does not violate the laws of justice, is left perfectly free to pursue his own interest his own way, and to bring both his industry and capital into competition with those of any other man, or order of men. The sovereign is completely discharged from a duty, in the attempting to perform which he must always be exposed to innumerable delusions, and for the proper performance of which no human wisdom or knowledge could ever be sufficient; the duty of superintending the industry of private people, and of directing it towards the employments most suitable to the interest of the society. According to the system of natural liberty, the sovereign has only three duties to attend to; three duties of great importance, indeed, but plain and intelligible to common understandings: first, the duty of protecting the society from the violence and invasion of other independent societies: secondly, the duty of protecting, as far as possible, every member of the society from the injustices or oppression of every other member of it, or the duty of establishing an exact administration of justice; and thirdly, the duty of erecting and maintaining certain public works and certain public institutions which it can never be for the interest of any individual, or small number of individuals, to erect and maintain; because the profit could never repay the expense to any individual or small number of individuals, though it may frequently do much more than repay it to a great society.

On Paying Taxes

The wars against France from 1793 to 1815 were financed mostly by government borrowing. Taxation did play a part, however, and income tax was introduced to supplement the traditional tax on land. The tax gained an immediate and lasting unpopularity. Taxpayers assessed themselves and there was widespread evasion. The income tax was particularly resented because it smacked of 'French slavery', object of much current xenophobic hatred. It should also be remembered that the Government servants who administered it were mostly political appointees as the tradition of impartial selection of civil servants by examination was half a century distant. The income tax was abolished in 1816 and successive governments did all they could to keep government expenditure as low as possible, while paying off the vastly inflated National Debt (which involved the new transfer of incomes from the labouring masses to the saving/investing middle and upper classes via indirect taxation on articles of common consumption like soap and candles). As far as growing industry was concerned the great benevolent feature of government taxation was that it left capital and profits alone, thus favouring accumulation and investment necessary for further economic growth.

DOCUMENT 18

Man Midwife, The further experiences of John Knyveton M.C., late Surgeon in the British Fleet during the years 1763-1809

January 12th 1799: This is a horrible war—the rapacity and greed of the

Government go beyond all limits—Parliament met on 20 November last year to consider the present financial position—not content with squeezing us dry in February 1798, it is now actually proposed to place A TAX ON INCOMES! No income under £60 per annum is to pay any duty at all, those from £100–105 a fortieth part and above £200 a tenth! It is a vile Jacobin, jumped up Jack-in-Office piece of impertinence—is a true Briton to have no privacy? Are the fruits of his labour and toil to be picked over, farthing by farthing, by the pimply minions of Bureaucracy?

Natural Laws and the Impossibility of Interference

Malthus' *Essay on Population* was probably the most influential work of this period, after *Wealth of Nations*. Its gloomy conclusion was that the growth of population would inexorably outrun the supply of food, leading to periodic crises of famine and disease which alone could restore equilibrium between numbers and subsistence. Malthus subsequently modified his views to show a number of ways in which this dilemma could be postponed (chiefly by postponement of marriage) but it was a simplified version of his thesis which exerted a powerful hold over the public mind of the nineteenth century, confirming their fatalistic passivity in the face of human misery and distress.

DOCUMENT 19

Thomas Robert Malthus, Essay on Population (1798) (1803 edn), pp 531–5

. . . There is one right, which man has generally been thought to possess, which I am confident he neither does, nor can, possess, a right to subsistence when his labour will not fairly purchase it. Our laws indeed say that he has this right, and bind the society to furnish employment and food to those who cannot get them in the regular market; but in so doing, they attempt to reverse the laws of nature. . . .

A man who is born into a world already possessed, if he cannot get subsistence from his parents on whom he has a just demand, and if the society do not want his labour, has no claim of right to the smallest portion of food, and in fact, has no business to be where he is. At nature's mighty feast there is no vacant cover for him. . . .

The poor are by no means inclined to be visionary. Their distresses are always real, though they are not attributed to the real causes. If these real causes were properly explained to them, and they were taught to know how small a part of their present distress was attributable to government, and how great a part to causes totally unconnected with it, discontent and irritation among the lower classes of people would show themselves much less frequently than at present.

The Role of Man

Smith's dictum that the untramelled exertions of the individual were the key to economic and social progress became the commonplace knowledge of the nineteenth century. Politicians of all shades of opinion were almost obliged to pay lip-service to the notion of laissez-faire and the doctrine itself began to seem vague and imprecise. Lord Macaulay was able to twist the concept in support of the Ten Hours Bill, which was fiercely resisted by manufacturing interests, in the name of laissez-faire. Regulation, it was being claimed by supporters of the Bill, was necessary to preserve the individual from exploitation which might sap the initiative and enterprise on which progress depended.

DOCUMENT 20

Thomas Babington Macaulay: Speech in the House of Commons, 22nd May 1846
Miscellaneous Writings and Speeches of Lord Macaulay (1882), pp 718–28

(Macaulay was speaking on the second reading of the Ten Hours Bill)

. . . What is it, Sir, that makes the great difference between country and country? Not the exuberance of the soil; not the mildness of climate; not mines, nor havens, nor rivers. These things are indeed valuable when put to their proper use by human intelligence: but human intelligence can do much without them; and they without human intelligence can do nothing. They exist in the highest degree in regions of which the inhabitants are few, and squalid, and barbarous, and naked, and starving; while on sterile rocks, amidst unwholesome marshes, and under inclement skies, may be found immense populations, well fed, well lodged, well clad, well governed. Nature meant Egypt and Sicily to be the gardens of the world. They once were so. Is it anything in the earth or in the air that makes Scotland more prosperous than Egypt, that makes Holland more prosperous than Sicily? No, it was the Scotchman that made Scotland, it was the Dutchman that made Holland. . . . Man, man is the great instrument that produces wealth. The natural difference between Campania and Spitzbergen is trifling, when compared with the difference between a country inhabited by men full of bodily and mental vigour, and a country inhabited by men sunk in bodily and mental decrepitude.

Self-Interest

DOCUMENT 21

Charles Dickens, Hard Times (1854)

A sunny midsummer day. There was such a thing sometimes, even in Coketown.

Seen from a distance in such weather, Coketown lay shrouded in a haze of its own, which appeared impervious to the sun's rays. You only knew the town was there, because you knew there could have been no such sulky blotch upon the prospect without a town. A blur of soot and smoke, now confusedly tending this way, now that way, now aspiring to the vault of Heaven, now murkily creeping along the earth, as the wind rose and fell, or changed its quarter: a dense formless jumble, with sheets of cross lights in it, that showed nothing but masses of darkness:—Coketown in the distance was suggestive of itself, though not a brick of it could be seen.

The wonder was, it was there at all. It had been ruined so often, that it was amazing how it had borne so many shocks. Surely there never was such fragile china-ware as that of which the millers of Coketown were made. Handle them never so lightly, and they fell to pieces with such ease that you might suspect them of having been flawed before. They were ruined when they were required to send labouring children to school: they were ruined when inspectors were appointed to look into their works; they were ruined when such inspectors considered it doubtful whether they were quite justified in chopping people up with their machinery; they were utterly undone when it was hinted that perhaps they need not always make quite so much smoke. Whenever a Coketowner felt he was ill-used—that is to say, whenever he was not left entirely alone, and it was proposed to hold him accountable for the consequences of any of his acts—he was sure to come out with the awful menace, that he 'would sooner pitch his property into the Atlantic'. This had terrified the Home Secretary within an inch of his life, on several occasions.

However, the Coketowners were so patriotic after all, that they never had pitched their property into the Atlantic yet, but, on the contrary, had been kind enough to take mighty good care of it. So there it was, in the haze yonder; and it increased and multiplied.

DOCUMENT 22

Samuel Smiles, Self-Help (1859)

One of the most strongly marked features of the English people is their spirit of industry, standing out prominent and distinct in their past history, and as strikingly characteristic of them now as at any former period. It is this spirit, displayed by the commons of England, which has laid the foundation and built up the industrial greatness of the empire. This vigorous growth of the nation has been mainly the result of the free energy of individuals, and it has been contingent upon the number of hands and minds from time to time actively employed within it, whether as cultivators of the soil, producers of articles of utility, contrivers of tools and machines, writers of books, or creators of works of art. And while this spirit of active industry has been the vital principle of the nation, it has also been the saving and remedial one, counteracting from time to time the effects of errors in our laws and imperfections in our constitution.

The career of industry which the nation has pursued, has also provided its best education. As steady application to work is the healthiest training for every individual, so it is the best discipline of state. Honourably industry travels the same road with duty, and Providence has closely linked both with happiness. The gods, says the poet, have placed labour and toil on the way leading to the Elysian fields. Certain it is that no bread eaten by man is so sweet as that earned by his own labour, whether bodily or mental. By labour the earth has been subdued, and man redeemed from barbarism; nor has a single step in civilisation been made without it. Labour is not only a necessity and a duty, but a blessing; only the idler feels it to be a curse. The duty of work is written on the thews and muscles of the limbs, the mechanism of the hand, the nerves and lobes of the brain—the sum of whose healthy action is satisfaction and enjoyment. In the school of labour is taught the best practical wisdom; nor is a life of manual employment, as we shall hereafter find, incompatible with high mental culture.

A De Tocqueville

Trade

England's Advantages for Trade

The expansion of British commerce dates from the sixteenth century. In the course of the seventeenth century, by war and commercial legislation, Britain had attained a supremacy over Holland as the common carrier of Europe, poised on the crossroads of the sea-lanes of North West Europe.

DOCUMENT 23

Chamberlayne, Magnae Britanniae Notitia (1708), I, p 42
Quoted in P. Mantowe, The Industrial Revolution, p 94

Our trade is the most considerable of the whole world, and indeed Great Britain is of all countries the most proper for trade, as well from its situation as an island as from the freedom and excellency of its constitution. . . .

Effects of Trade on Britain

Trade enjoyed considerable prestige in Britain. It was felt to perform a service to the state and employment in trading ventures was not beneath the dignity of the younger sons of great noble houses. Trading wealth and landed wealth were already marrying, both in the commercial and in the literal sense.

DOCUMENT 24

R. Campbell on the importance of commerce (The London Tradesman, 1747)
Quoted in English Historical Documents, Vol X

. . . The Trades we have been hitherto speaking of, are confined to one Place, one City or Country; but Commerce, the Sphere of the Merchant, extends itself to all the known World, and gives Life and Vigour to the whole Machine. Some Tradesmen we have treated of employ several different Branches, some particular Crafts dependant on them; but the Merchant employs them all, sets the whole Society at work, supplies them with Materials to fabricate their Goods, and vends their Manufactures in the most distant Corners of the Globe. Other Arts, Crafts and Mysteries live upon one another, and never add one Sixpence to the aggregate Wealth of the Kingdom; but the Merchant draws his honest Gain from the distant Poles, and every Shilling he returns more than he carried out, adds so much to the National Riches and Capital Stock of the Kingdom. Wherever he comes, wherever he lives, Wealth and Plenty follow him: The Poor is set to work, Manufactures flourish, Poverty is banished, and Public Credit increases. The Advantages of Commerce is evident to all Mankind; the wisest, the politest Nations on Earth now court her to their Dominions: The *Dutch* and us are two pregnant Proofs of the Power and Advantages of Traffic. Before we were a Trading People, we were, it is true, subsisted by the natural Produce of the Island; but we lived in a kind of Penury, a Stranger to Money or Affluence, inconsiderable in ourselves, and of no Consequence to our Neighbours: Our Manners were rude, our Knowledge of the World trifling; Politeness was a Stranger at our Courts; Ignorance and barbarous Simplicity spread their Empire over the whole Island: But we no sooner became a Trading People, than the Arts and Sciences began to revive, and polished us out of our rustic Simplicity and Ignorance; the People found out new Means of supplying their Wants, and the Nation in general accumulated Riches at Home, and commanded Respect abroad; a new Scene of Power started out of Commerce, and the wide Ocean owned the Sovereignty of Imperial Britain.

Trade and Politics

By the mid-eighteenth century trade, largely in the hands of great companies like the Hudson Bay or East India Companies, was a powerful political lobby and the territorial spoils of war which Britain gained in the course of the century were selected for their commercial rather than their purely strategic value.

DOCUMENT 25

John Campbell, The Present State of Europe (1750)
Quoted in English Historical Documents, Vol X

There is a Distinction often made, chiefly by Foreigners, between the Interest and the Commerce of Great Britain; but in reality this is a Distinction without a Difference; for the Interest and Commerce of the *British* Empire are so inseparably united, that they may be very well considered as one and the same. For Commerce is that tie, by which the several, and even the most distant Parts of this Empire, are connected and kept together, so as to be rendred [*sic*] Parts of the same whole, and to receive not only Countenance and Protection, but Warmth and Nourishment from the vital

Parts of our Government of which, if I may be indulged so figurative an Expression, our Monarchy is the Head, and our Liberty the Soul. Whatever therefore assists, promotes, and extends our Commerce, is consistent with our Interest, and whatever weakens, impairs or circumscribes it, is repugnant thereto.

Evils of Tariffs

Adam Smith denounced the system of tariffs by which each nation sought to protect its industry from its rivals and emphasised the mutual benefits which would follow if each nation concentrated its efforts on producing those goods which its natural resources made it best fitted to produce. His ideas won enthusiastic supporters, including the Prime Minister, Pitt, who claimed that Smith's book would rule the next generation. The Eden treaty of 1786 took a small step towards implementing its recommendations by reducing tariffs between England and France. The outbreak of war in 1793 set the cause of Free Trade back 30 years.

DOCUMENT 26

Adam Smith, Wealth of Nations (1776), Vol II, p 401-2

If a foreign country can supply us with a commodity cheaper than we ourselves can make it, better buy it of them with some part of the produce of our own industry employed in a way in which we have some advantage. The general industry of the country, being always in proportion to the capital which employs it, will not thereby be diminished; but only left to find out the way in which it can be employed with the greatest advantage. It is certainly not employed to the greatest advantage when it is thus directed towards an object which it can buy cheaper than it can make. The value of its annual produce is certainly more or less diminished when it is thus turned away from producing commodities evidently of more value than the commodity which it is directed to produce. According to the supposition, that a commodity could be purchased from foreign countries cheaper than it can be made at home, it could, therefore, have been purchased with a part only of the commodities, or, what is the same thing, with a part only of the price of the commodities, which the industry employed by an equal capital would have produced at home, had it been left to follow its natural course. The industry of the country, therefore, is thus turned away from a more to a less advantageous employment, and the exchangeable value of its annual produce, instead of being increased, according to the intention of the lawgiver, must necessarily be diminished by every such regulation.

Complexity of Protective Legislation

The laws which governed British commerce at the end of the French wars were the residue of centuries of effort to protect this or that industry or trade or spite this or that enemy or ally. Free Trade doctrine was gaining ground, particularly amongst members of the Board of Trade, but it was still unacceptable to many merchants, bred in the tradition of protection and made cautious by the upsets and uncertainties of the war and post-war period.

DOCUMENT 27

Report from the Select Committee of the House of Commons on the means of maintaining and improving the foreign trade of the country, 18th July 1820 Quoted in English Historical Documents, Vol XI

. . . .Your committee . . . are anxious to call the observation of the House to the excessive accumulation and complexity of the laws under which the commerce of the country is regulated. . . . These laws, passed at different periods, and many of them arising out of temporary circumstances, amount . . . to upwards of 2,000; of which no less than 1,100 were in force in the year 1815, and many additions have been since made. After such a statement it will not appear extraordinary that it should be a matter of complaint to the British merchant, that so far from the course in which he is to guide his transactions being plain and simple; so far from being able to undertake his operations, and to avail himself of favourable openings as they arise, with promptitude and confidence, he is frequently reduced to the necessity of resorting to the services of professional advisers, to ascertain what he may venture to do and what he must avoid, before he is able to embark on his commercial adventures with the assurance of being secure from the consequences of an infringement of the law. . . . Perhaps no service more valuable could be rendered to the trade of the Empire . . . than an accurate revision of this vast and confused mass of legislation, and the establishment of some certain, simple and consistent principles, to which all the regulations of commerce might be referred, and under which the transactions of merchants . . . might be conducted with facility, with safety, and with confidence.

An Expanding Port

Despite the confused mass of legislation which hampered British commerce, British ports, served by increasingly sophisticated transport systems, grew on the flood of imported raw materials necessary to sustain the expansion of British manufacture. Alexis de Tocqueville, the French historian, was amazed at the runaway growth of Liverpool, which by 1850 was handling a greater volume of commerce than London itself.

DOCUMENT 28

A. de Tocqueville, Journey to England (1835)

Liverpool. Town destined to become the centre of English trade. A fisherman's harbour three centuries ago. A small town sixty years ago. The slave trade, basis of its commercial greatness. It carried slaves to the Spanish colonies at better prices than all the others. The foundation of the United States, the manufacturing development of Manchester and Birmingham, and the spread of English trade over the whole world have done the rest. Conversation with M. Laine, French Consul at Liverpool.

Q. English industry, which I had imagined to be stationary, seems to be growing fast.

A. Yes. It is undertaking ever greater developments.

Q. Liverpool is growing the whole time?

A. Incredibly fast. Everything goes at a run. The railway will further speed up the rate at which London can be by-passed as a sea-port. Already London deals almost only with European trade, and soon the trade of Northern Europe will pass through Liverpool, Hull and Derby. Probably in ten years Liverpool's commercial power will be greater than that of London.

Cobden on Free Trade

The commercial upsets of 1836–9 and the simultaneous disasters in foreign policy brought the Whig government to the verge of bankruptcy. The crisis deepened with the turn of the decade and Peel's Tory administration was elected to restore the nation's finances and set the nation back on the road to prosperity. Chartist agitation was at its height in 1842, and, fearful of revolution, the middle classes were ready to tolerate radical measures. Peel supplied them. He set about abolishing or reducing a whole range of tariffs with the aim of simplifying revenue collection and encouraging trade in products which had in effect been banned by the high import duties placed upon them. Set upon this radical course, which led him to extend state control over the railways and the Bank of England, he found himself further and further pressed by the arguments and agitation of the Anti-Corn Law League, which was devoted to securing the abolition of the legislation which, it was thought, protected the agricultural interest at the expense of the nation, by maintaining the price of corn at an artificially high level. Orators like Cobden and Bright, aided by the railways, the new Penny Post and cheap steam-printed literature, put the League's case with powerful simplicity:

DOCUMENT 29

Richard Cobden: Speech in London, 8th February 1844
Bright and Rogers, Speeches of Richard Cobden, M.P. (1870), Vol I,
pp 118–33

I am a manufacturer of clothing, and I do not know why, in this climate, and in the artificial state of society in which we live, the making of clothes should not be as honourable—because it is pretty near as useful—a pursuit as the manufacture of food. Well, did you ever hear any debates in the House to fix the price of my commodities in the market? Suppose we had a majority of cotton-printers (which happens to be my manufacture) in the House. . . . Let us suppose that you were reading the newspaper some fine morning and saw an account of a majority in the House have been engaged the night before in fixing the price at which yard-wide prints should be sold: 'Yard-wide prints, of such a quality, 10d. a yard; of such a quality, 9d; of such a quality, 8d; of such a quality, 7d;' and so on. Why, you would rub your eyes with astonishment! . . . Now, did it ever occur to you that there is no earthly difference between a body of men, manufacturers of corn, sitting down in the House, and passing a law enacting that wheat shall be so much, barley so much, beans so much, and oats so much?

Our opponents tell us that our object in bringing about the repeal of the Corn-laws is, by reducing the price of corn, to lower the rate of their wages. I can only answer upon this point for the manufacturing districts; but, as far as they are concerned, I state it most emphatically as a truth, that, for the last twenty years, whenever corn has been cheap wages have been high in Lancashire; and, on the other hand, when bread has been dear wages have been greatly reduced. . . .

Now, let me be fully understood as to what Free Traders really do want. We do not want cheap corn merely in order that we may have low money prices. What we desire is plenty of corn, and we are utterly careless what its price is, provided we obtain it at the natural price. All we ask is this, that corn shall follow the same law which the monopolists in food admit that labour must follow; that 'it shall find its natural level in the markets of the world' . . .

To pay for that corn, more manufactures would be required from this country; this would lead to an increased demand for labour in the manu-facturing districts, which would necessarily be attended with a rise in wages, in order that the goods might be made for the purpose of exchanging for the corn brought from abroad. . . . I observe there are narrow-minded men in the agricultural districts, telling us, 'Oh, if you allow Free Trade, and bring in a quarter of corn from abroad, it is quite clear that you will sell one quarter less in England'. . . . What! I would ask, if you set more people to work at better wages—if you can clear your streets of those spectres which are now haunting your thoroughfares begging their daily bread—if you can depopulate your workhouses and clear off the two million of paupers which now exist in the land, and put them to work at productive industry—do you not think that they would consume some of the wheat as well as you; and may not they be as we are now, consumers of wheaten bread by millions, instead of existing on their present miserable dietary? . . .

With free trade in corn, so far from throwing land out of use or injuring the cultivation of the poorer soils, free trade in corn is the very way to increase the production at home, and stimulate the cultivation of the poorer soils by compelling the application of more capital and labour to them. We do not contemplate deriving one quarter less corn from the soil of this country; we do not anticiapte having one pound less of butter or cheese, or one head less of cattle or sheep: we expect to have a great increase in pro-duction and consumption at home; but all we contend for is this, that when we, the people here, have purchased all that can be raised at home, we shall be allowed to go 3,000 miles—to Poland, Russia or America—for more; and that there shall be no let or hindrance put in the way of our getting this additional quantity.

Free Trade—The Moral Aspect

Free Trade acquired moral overtones, which made it attractive to those who wanted a gospel of spiritual as well as material progress. It was preached with the fervour of religion, but it was the disastrous European famine of 1845–6, which struck potato-fed Ireland with awful ferocity, which finally pushed Peel to the logic of total repeal of the Corn Laws in 1846, a decision which shattered his own agrarian-based party.

DOCUMENT 30

Bright and Rogers, Speeches of Richard Cobden, M.P. (1870), Vol. I, p 79

Free Trade! What is it? Why, breaking down the barriers that separate nations; those barriers, behind which nestle the feelings of pride, revenge, hatred and jealousy, which every now and then burst their bounds and deluge whole countries with blood; those feelings which nourish the poison of war and conquest, which assert that without conquest we can have no trade, which foster that lust for conquest and dominion which sends forth your warrior chiefs to scatter devastation through other lands, and then calls them back that they may be enthroned securely in your passions, but only to harass and oppress you at home. It is because I think I have a full apprehension of the moral bearing of this question, that I take pride and gratification in forming one in the present agitation.'

Trade and Foreign Investment

The French Wars (1793–1815) destroyed Amsterdam's position as Europe's financial capital; at the same time the expansion of the National Debt in England stimulated the development of a sophisticated financial system and created a large class of rentiers, living off investments. The reconstruction of Europe after 1815 and the exploitation of newly-independent South America offered the first fields for foreign investment by Britain's prospering middle class, which was receiving far more than its proportionate share of the nation's growing wealth, and which sought profitable outlets for its idle capital.

DOCUMENT 31

G. R. Porter, Progress of the Nation, p 627

A very large amount of capital belonging to individuals in this country, the result of their savings, has of late years sought profitable investment in other lands. It has been computed that the United States of America have absorbed in this manner more than twenty-five millions of English capital, which sum has been invested in various public undertakings, such as canals, railroads, and banks in that country. Large sums have also been, from time to time, invested in the public securities of that and other foreign governments—not always, indeed, with a profitable result.

When the security thus accepted proves good, there can be no reasonable objection made to this course. We may feel quite sure that capital would not thus be sent abroad but with the reasonable expectation of obtaining for its use a greater return than could be secured at home, and by such means the accumulation of property is accelerated. Besides the ultimate advantage, there results this present good from the transmission of our savings to other lands, that it sets in motion the springs of industry to provide the means for that transmission. It is not money, in the usual acceptation of the word, that thus finds its way abroad for investment, but products and manufactures, the results of British industry. We have no surplus bullion out of which such advances could be made, and even if we had, it would not be profitable to us thus to dispose of it. It may be in insulated cases, and under temporary influences, that bullion is exported for such a purpose at times when we cannot very well spare it, but even then the evil is soon remedied through the ordinary and well-understood operations, either direct or indirect of commerce.

Transport

Roads

Turnpikes

Daniel Defoe, renowned as the author of *Robinson Crusoe*, was a professional journalist and pamphleteer and an acute observer of the contemporary scene. (His *Tour* is available in a 2-volume Everyman edition.) The first turnpike was set up at Wadesmill, in Hertfordshire, in 1663 and this system of road maintenance spread over most of the country in the following century.

DOCUMENT 32

Daniel Defoe, Tour through the Whole Island of Great Britain, 1724-7

ORIGINS AND BENEFITS OF TURNPIKES

... the soil of all the midland part of England, even from sea to sea, is of a deep stiff clay, ... and it carries a bredth of near 50 miles at least, in some places much more; nor is it possible to go from London to any part of Britain, north, without crossing this clayey dirty part.

... The reason of my taking notice of the badness of the roads, through all the midland counties, is this; that these are counties which drive a very great trade with the city of London, and with one another, perhaps the greatest of any counties in England; and that, by consequence, the carriage is exceeding great and also that all the land carriage of the northern counties necessarily goes through these counties, so the roads had been plow'd so deep, and materials have been in some places so difficult to be had for repair of roads, that all the surveyors rates have been able to do nothing; nay, the very whole country has not been able to repair them; that is to say, it was a burthen too great for the poor farmers; for in England it is the tenant, not the landlord, that pays the surveyors of the highways.

This necessarily brought the country to bring these things before Parliament; and the consequence has been, that turnpikes or toll-bars have been set up on the several great roads of England, beginning at London, and proceeding through almost all those dirty deep roads, in the midland counties especially; at which turnpikes all carriages, droves of cattle, and travellers on horseback, are oblig'd to pay an easy toll; that is to say, a horse a penny, a coach three pence, a cart four pence, at some six pence to eight pence, a waggon six pence, in some a shilling, and the like; cattle pay by the score, or by the head, in some places more, in some places less; but in no place is it thought a burthen that I ever met with, the benefit of a good road abundantly making amends for that little charge the travellers are put to at the turnpikes.

Several of these turnpikes and tolls had been set up of late years, and great progress had been made in mending the most difficult ways, and that with such success as well deserves a place in this account; And this is one reason for taking notice of it in this manner; for as the memory of the Romans which is so justly famous, is preserv'd in nothing more visible to common observation, than in the remains of those noble causeways and highways, which they made through all parts of the kingdom, and which were found so needful, even then, when there was not the five hundredth part of the commerce and carriage that is now: How much more valuable must these new works be, tho' nothing to compare with those of the Romans, for the firmness and duration of their work?

. . . 'tis more than probable, that our posterity may see the roads all over England restor'd in their time to such a perfection, that travelling and carriage of goods will be much more easy both to man and horse, than ever it was since the Romans lost this island. Nor will the charge be burthensome to any body; as for trade, it will be encourag'd by this every way; for carriage of all kinds of heavy goods will be much easier; the waggoners will either perform in less time, or draw heavier loads, or the same load with fewer horses; the pack-horse will carry heavier burthens, or travel farther in a day, and so perform their journey in less time; all which will tend to lessen the rate of carriage, and so bring goods cheaper to market. The fat cattle will drive lighter, and come to market with less toil, and consequently both go farther in one day, and not waste their flesh, and heat and spoil themselves, in wallowing thro' the mud and sloughs as is now the case. The sheep will be able to travel in the winter, and the city not be obliged to give great prizes to the butchers for mutton, because it cannot be brought up out of Leicestershire and Lincolnshire, the sheep not being able to travel. . . .

Another benefit of these new measures for repairing the roads by turn-pikes, is the opening of drains and water-courses, and building bridges especially over the smaller waters, which are oftentimes the most dangerous to travellers on hasty rains, and always most injurious to the roads, by lying in holes and puddles, to the great spoiling the bottom, and making constant sloughs, sometimes able to bury both man and horse. . . . To give an eminent instance of it, we refer the curious to take the road from Blackman-street in Southwark, to Croydon, for an example, where, if we are not mistaken, he will find eleven bridges wholly new-built in ten miles length. . . .

This improving of the roads is an infinite improvement to the towns near London, in the convenience of coming to them, which makes the citizens flock out in greater numbers than ever to take lodgings and country-houses, which many, whose business call'd them often to London, could not do, because of the labour of riding forward and backward, when the roads were but a little dirty, and this is seen in the difference in the rents of houses in those villages upon such repair'd roads, from the rents of the like dwellings and lodgings in other towns of equal distance where they want those helps, and particularly the increase of the number of buildings in those towns, as above.

The benefit of these turnpikes appears now to be so great, and the people in all places being to be so sensible of it, that it is incredible what effect it has already had upon trade in the countries where it is more compleatly finish'd; even the carriage of goods is abated in some places, 6d per hundredweight, in some places 12d per hundred, which is abundantly more advantage to commerce, than the charge paid amounts to, and yet at the same time the expense is paid by the carriers too, who make the abatement; so that the benefit in abating the rate of carriage is wholly and simply the tradesmen's, not the carriers.

Yet the advantage is evident to the carriers also another way; for, as was observ'd before, they can bring more weight with the same number of horses, nor are their horses so hard work'd and fatigued with their labour as they were before. . . .

The advantage to all other kinds of travelling I omit here; such as the safety and ease to gentlemen travelling up to London on all occasions whether to the term, or to Parliament, to Court, or on any other necessary occasion, which is not a small part of the benefit of these new methods.

Effects of Improved Roads

The spectacular achievements of the canal-builders eclipse the less applauded work of the turnpike trusts, which made a vital contribution to the efficient transport of goods and passengers over short and long distances, reducing travelling times from days to hours and enabling the Royal Mail coaches (instituted by William Palmer of Bath in 1784) to operate schedules timed to the minute.

DOCUMENT 33

Homer Enquiry into the Means of Preserving and Improving the Publick Roads (1767), pp 7–8
Quoted in Jackman, Development of Transportation in Modern England, p 300

Dispatch, which is the very life and soul of business, becomes daily more attainable by the free circulation opening in every channel, which is adapted to it. Merchandise and manufactures find a ready conveyance to the markets. . . . There never was a more astonishing revolution accomplished in the internal system of any country, than has been within a few years in that of England. The carriage of grain, coals, merchandise, etc. is in general conducted with little more than half the number of horses with which it formerly was. Journies of business are performed with more than double expedition. Improvements in agriculture keep pace with those of trade. Everything wears the face of dispatch; every article of our produce becomes more valuable; and the hinge which had guided all these movements, and upon which they turn, is the reformation which has been made in our public roads.

Continued Improvement of Roads

The turnpikes provided the routes and maintained the surface of the highway, but until J. L. Macadam's system became popular in the early nineteenth century, their work was unsystematic and wasteful of labour and materials. Macadam stressed the importance of a sound road-bed, for it was the sub-soil, not the surface, which bore the actual weight of the traffic. The road surface, cambered to drain off rain-water, was meant to serve as a roof or umbrella over the foundation. Macadam's roads necessitated a large initial outlay but very little subsequent maintenance.

By the time his principles had been universally applied the railway was becoming a more popular mode of long-distance travel.

DOCUMENT 34

G. R. Porter, Progress of the Nation, p 291

The chief improvement made of late years in England in regard to turnpike roads, has consisted in reconstructing them upon more scientific principles than were previously employed, an advantage which is mainly owing to the exertions of the late Mr M'Adam, whose plans have been adopted generally throughout the kingdom, as well as in several foreign countries. England had long been provided with roads in every quarter; yet we find, from Parliamentary returns, that, between 1818 and 1829, the length of turnpike-roads in England and Wales increased by more than one thousand miles . . . but this increase is of little importance if viewed comparatively with the improvements introduced in their construction and management.

Canals

The Duke of Bridgewater's Canal

The Duke of Bridgewater's canal ran between the Duke's coal mines at Worsley and the growing manufacturing town of Manchester. It took five years to complete the first section and it cost a quarter of a million pounds, but it slashed transport costs so that the price of coal in Manchester was halved.

DOCUMENT 35

An Account of the Duke of Bridgewater's new inland navigation
Annual Register (1763)

Manchester, September 30th

Sir,

I have lately been viewing the artificial wonders of London, and the natural wonders of the Peaks; but none of them gave me so much pleasure as the Duke of Bridgewater's navigation, in this country. His projector, the ingenious Mr Brindley, has indeed made such improvements in this way as are truly astonishing. At Barton bridge he has erected a navigable canal in the air; for it is as high as the tops of the trees. Whilst I was surveying it with a mixture of wonder and delight, four barges passed me in the space of about three minutes, two of them being chained together, and dragged by two horses, who went on the terras of the canal, whereon, I must own, I durst hardly venture to walk, as I almost trembled to behold the large river Irwell underneath me, across which this navigation is carried by a bridge. . . .

This navigation begins at the foot of some hills, in which the Duke's coals are dug, from whence a canal is cut through rocks, which daylight never enters. By this means large boats are hauled to the innermost parts of those hills, and being there filled with coals, are brought out by an easy current, which supplies the whole navigation for the space of about ten miles . . .

From Barton I steered my course towards this place and in my way sometimes saw the navigation carried over public roads, in some places over bogs, but generally by the side of hills. . . .

Channels are now cutting also in many other coal-pits, and boats are used instead of wheel-barrows, to convey the coals to the mouths of the pits; nay, it is even said that some Dutch engineers are coming over hither to perfect themselves in the art of inland navigation.

The Potential Value of Canals

The success of the Duke of Bridgewater's canal prompted other landowners to imitate his example and pool their savings to finance construction of canals which would, they hoped, develop the areas through which they ran by bringing them into contact with new urban markets. The joint-stock company established by private Act of Parliament became a popular device for accumulating capital and there were two major bursts of speculation and construction, in the 1770s and the 1790s. At the end Britain had about 2,500 miles of canal at a modest cost of £25,000,000.

DOCUMENT 36

John Campbell, A Political Survey of Britain (1774)
Quoted in English Historical Documents, Vol X

... As soon therefore as it appeared, that an easy and commodious Passage could be opened between Manchester and Liverpool, all Diffidence and all Difficulties vanished. Surveys were immediately directed; and, as soon as they were perfected, Subscriptions chearfully followed, the Nobility and Gentry expressing the warmest Zeal in risquing their private Property for the publick Service. But then this Zeal was according to Knowledge; they were clearly convinced of the Utility of the Undertaking; and they saw, without suffering any Uneasiness, that Time, Labour, and Expence, must purchase them those Benefits this new Navigation was to bestow; and therefore what in Days of less Industry, less Commercial Spirit, and, let us add, less Opulence, would have been held insuperable Obstacles, did not at all deter them from pursuing so great and so glorious a Design.

WHAT the actual Advantages, that will be derived from these Canals when finished, may be, Time and Experience only can determine; but upon what reasonable Expectations they have been so steadily as well as strenuously supported, is incumbent upon me to report, in order to justify the Pains taken about them in this Work. It is a vast Tract of Country through which they are to pass, and not barely one or two, but several Counties that are to share the Benefit of them, with this remarkable Circumstance in their Favour, that in no Part of this noble Island could such a Communication be of more Use, the Number considered of large, and many of them manufacturing Towns, in its Vicinity. All Kinds of Provisions, but more especially Grain, will by their means be rendered cheaper, and kept to a more equal Price. For by furnishing Manure from great Distances at a low Rate, and giving a quick Carriage even to remote Markets, the Canal will excite an active Spirit of Cultivation, and the Certainty of obtaining a speedy Supply at a small Expence will render an unreasonable Rise of Corn, where it has been in Times past frequently and fatally experienced, for the future in a great measure impracticable. Many bulky, but at the same time very useful Commodities, such as Flint, Free, Lime, Mill, Grinding, and Paving Stones, Marl, Slate, Coals of different Kinds, Marble, Alabaster, Iron Ore, will find a much easier and cheaper Passage, and of course reach many more and those too better Markets, than they can be carried to, circumstances as they are at present.

FREQUENT Additions will probably be made to these natural Riches from the Discoveries that must arise from the cutting through a Variety of Soils in the Progress of this great Work, some Instances of which have occurred already. Besides, the Staples of these several Counties may be carried farther, in great Quantities, and be notwithstanding afforded at lower Rates, such as Timber from different Parts of Lancashire, the Salt and Cheese of Cheshire, Earthen-ware from Staffordshire, numerous Articles from Birmingham, and all the various Manufactures from Manchester and other Places, will be relieved from a Variety of Impediments under which they have hitherto laboured. Raw Materials of every Sort will be conveyed with much more Ease and Expedition to the several Towns where they are wrought up, and, when manufactured, will with like Facility be carried to the Ports from which they are usually shipped, either Coast-ways to different Parts of this, or into other Countries. Thus Agriculture, Manufactures, domestic Trade, foreign Commerce, and every Species of Industry subservient to all these, will be evidently and in a high Degree promoted by this Inland Navigation, to say nothing of the Numbers who will live and be comfortably subsisted by it. . . .

Extension of Canals

Canals brought new possibilities to landlocked centres of manufacture, particularly the West Midlands, by bringing them into easy contact with export markets, and by a network of navigable waterways, with every major port and city in England.

DOCUMENT 37

Arthur Young on the industrial development of Birmingham (1791)
Quoted in English Historical Documents, Vol X

The capital improvement wrought since I was here before is the canal to Oxford, Coventry, Wolverhampton, &c.; the port, as it may be called, or double canal head in the town crowded with coal barges is a noble spectacle, with that prodigious animation, which the immense trade of this place could alone give. I looked around me with amazement at the change effected in twelve years; so great that this place may now probably be reckoned, with justice, the first manufacturing town in the world. From this port and these quays you may now go by water to Hull, Liverpool, Bristol, Oxford (130 miles) and London. The cut was opened through the coal mines to Wolverhampton in 1769. In 1783, into the new mines of Wednesbury, and to the junction with the Coventry canal, at Faseley, near Tamworth.

Impact of Railways on Canals

The advent of the railways in the 1830s and 1840s brought a sudden demise to many canals. Some, chiefly those built in the agricultural south, had never known prosperity, but others had paid high dividends for years. Split between large numbers of proprietors the canals were unable to present a united front to the railways and by the 1860s the majority has been acquired by railway companies who allowed them to fall into disrepair.

DOCUMENT 38

Select Committee on the Amalgamation of Railways and Canals (1846)
Quoted in English Historical Documents, Vol XII

On the introduction of railways . . . the consequent competition materially reduced the expense of conveyance. Instances have been adduced before your Committee in which the charges for the conveyance of merchandise have been lowered by these means to one-seventh of their former amount, and there are now few parts of the country which have not derived material advantage from the competition between railroads and canals.

Railways

Railways were common long before locomotives. Parallel tracks joined many mines and quarries to rivers and canals before the beginning of the nineteenth century, when Trevithick's experiments with high-pressure steam made the locomotive a practical proposition. In the North-East mining area, where localised transport problems were most acute, a colliery engine man, George Stephenson, gained a reputation for his skill in constructing colliery engines and tracks. He was invited to supervise the construction of the Stockton and Darlington railway which opened in 1825, using locomotives to haul freight but using horses to haul passenger coaches. Stephenson then constructed the Liverpool and Manchester railway which ran for 30 miles across difficult ground and was the largest engineering venture ever attempted to date. It was opened in 1830 and was an immediate and lasting success.

Liverpool-Manchester Railway Prospectus
Quoted in English Historical Documents, Vol XI

The Committee of the Liverpool and Manchester Railroad Company think it right to state, concisely, the grounds upon which they rest their claims to public encouragement and support.

The importance, to a commercial state, of a safe and cheap mode of transit for merchandise . . . will be readily acknowledged. This was the plea upon the first introduction of canals: it was for the public advantage; and although the new mode of conveyance interfered with existing and inferior modes, and was opposed to the feelings and prejudices of landholders, the great principle of the public good prevailed, and experience has justified the decision.

It is upon the same principle that railroads are now proposed to be established; as a means of conveyance manifestly superior to existing modes; possessing, moreover, this recommendation in addition to what could have been claimed in favour of canals namely, that the railroad scheme holds out to the public not only a cheaper, but far more expeditious conveyance than any yet established. . . .

The ground has been surveyed by eminent engineers and the estimated expense of a railroad, upon the most improved construction, including the charge for locomotive engines to be employed on the line, and other contingencies, is £400,000, which sum it is proposed to raise in 4,000 shares of £100 each.

The total quantity of merchandise passing between Liverpool and Manchester is estimated, by the lowest computation, at one thousand tons per day. The bulk of this merchandise is transported either by the Duke of Bridgewater's canal or the 'Mersey and Irwell Navigation'. By both of these conveyances goods must pass up the river Mersey, a distance of 16 or 18 miles, subject to serious delays from contrary winds, and not infrequently, to actual loss or damage from tempestuous weather. The average length of passage by these conveyances including the customary detention on the wharfs, may be taken at 36 hours. . . . The average charge upon merchandise for the last fourteen years has been about fifteen shillings per ton.

By the projected railroad, the transit of merchandise between Liverpool and Manchester will be effected in four or five hours, and the charge to the merchant will be reduced at least one third. Here, then, will be accomplished an immense pecuniary saving to the public, over and above what is perhaps still more important, the *economy of time*. . . .

The committee are aware that it will not be immediately understood by the public how the proprietors of a railroad, requiring an invested capital of £400,000, can afford to carry goods at so great a reduction upon the charge of the present water companies. . . . It is not that the water companies have not been able to carry goods on more reasonable terms, but that, strong in the enjoyment of their monopoly, they have not thought proper to do so. . . . IT IS COMPETITION THAT IS WANTED. . . .

The present canal establishments are inadequate to . . . the regular and punctual conveyance of goods at all periods and seasons. In summer time there is frequently a deficiency of water, obliging boats to go only half-loaded . . . while, in winter, they are sometimes locked up with frosts, for weeks together. . . . In the present state of trade and of commercial enterprise, dispatch is no less essential than economy. Merchandise is frequently brought across the Atlantic from New York to Liverpool in twenty-one days: while, owing to the various causes of delay above enumerated, goods have in some instances been longer on their passage from Liverpool to Manchester. . . .

The immediate and prominent advantages to be anticipated from the proposed railroad are, increased facilities to the general operations of commerce . . . as well as an immense pecuniary saving to the trading community. But the inhabitants at large of these populous towns will reap their full share of direct and immediate benefit. Coals will be brought to market in greater plenty and at a reduced price; and farming produce, of various kinds, will find its way from greater distances and at more reasonable rates. To the landholders, also, in the vicinity of the line, the railroad offers important advantages in extensive markets for their mineral and agricultural produce, as well as in a facility of obtaining lime and manure at a cheap rate in return. Moreover, as a cheap and expeditious means of conveyance for travellers, the railway holds out the prospect of a public accommodation, the magnitude and importance of which cannot be immediately ascertained.
29 October 1824.'

A First Railway Journey

The public soon lost its fear of steam travel and passenger travel provided a greater proportion of railway receipts before 1850 than freight, for which the railways had originally been constructed. The success of the Liverpool and Manchester sparked off a railway 'mania' in the 1830s, which laid the trunk routes between the major towns. A larger mania in the 1840s brought the total invested in railways to £250,000,000 and by 1851 6,800 miles of track had been completed.

Diary, Reminiscences and Correspondence of Henry Crabb Robinson (1833)
ed. T. Sadler (1872), ii, pp 138–9

Liverpool 10 June—At twelve I got upon an omnibus and was driven up
a steep hill to the place where the steam-carriages start. We travelled in the
second class of carriages. There were five carriages linked together, in each
of which were placed open seats for the traveller, four and four facing each
other; but not all were full; and, besides, there was a close carriage, and also
a machine for luggage. The fare was four shillings for the thirty-one miles.
Everything went on so rapidly that I had scarcely the power of observation.
The road begins at an excavation through rock, and is to a certain extent
insulated from the adjacent country. It is occasionally placed on bridges,
and frequently intersected by ordinary roads. Not quite a perfect level is
preserved. On setting off there is a slight jolt, arising from the chain catching
each carriage, but, once in motion we proceeded as smoothly as possible.
For a minute or two the pace is gentle, and is constantly varying. The machine
produces little smoke or steam. First in order is the tall chimney; then the
boiler, a barrel-like vessel; then an oblong reservoir of water; then a vehicle
for coals; and then comes, of a length infinitely extendible, the train of
carriages. If all the seats had been filled, our train would have carried about
150 passengers; but a gentleman assured me at Chester that he went with
a thousand persons to Newton fair. There must have been two engines
then. I have heard since that two thousand persons and more went to and
from the fair that day. But two thousand only, at three shillings each way
would have produced £600! But after all, the expense is so great that it
is considered uncertain whether the establishment will ultimately remunerate
the proprietors. Yet I have heard that it already yields the shareholders a
dividend of nine per cent. And Bills have passed for making railroads
between London and Birmingham, and Birmingham and Liverpool. What a
change will it produce in the intercourse! One conveyance will take between
100 and 200 passengers, and the journey will be made in a forenoon! Of
the rapidity of the journey I had bitter experience on my return; but I may
say now that, stoppages included, it may certainly be made at the rate of
twenty miles an hour!

The Threat of the Railways

J. Francis, A History of the English Railway (1851), i, pp 119–20

What was to be done with all those who have advanced money in making
and repairing turnpike roads? What was to become of the coach-makers
and harness-makers, coach masters, coach-men, inn-keepers, horse-breeders

and horse-dealers? The beauty and comfort of country gentlemen's estates would be destroyed by it. Was the House aware of the smoke and the noise, the hiss and the whirl which locomotive engines, passing at the rate of ten or twelve miles an hour, would occasion? Neither the cattle ploughing in the fields or grazing in the meadows could behold them without dismay. Lease-holders and tenants, agriculturalists, graziers and dairy-men would all be in arms . . . Iron would be raised in price one hundred per cent; or, more probably, it would be exhausted altogether. It would be the greatest nuisance, the most complete disturbance of quiet and comfort in all parts of the kingdom, that the ingenuity of man could invent.

Impact of the Railways

DOCUMENT 42

The Economist, 1851
Quoted in E. Royston Pike, Human Documents of the Victorian Golden Age

STUPENDOUS PROGRESS IN LOCOMOTION

. . . In 1829 the first railway for the transport of passengers was opened between Liverpool and Manchester;—it opened at the modest speed of 20 miles an hour. At the period at which we write, the whole of England is traversed by almost countless railways in every direction. In the days of Adam the average speed of travel, if Adam ever did such things, was four miles an hour . . . in the year 1828, or *4,000 years afterwards it was still only ten miles*, and sensible and scientific men were ready to affirm and eager to prove that this rate could never be materially exceeded;—in 1850, it is habitually forty miles an hour, and *seventy* for those who like it. We have reached in a single bound from the speed of a horse's canter, to the utmost speed comparable with the known strength and coherence of brass and iron.

Now, who have specially benefited by this vast invention? The rich, whose horses and carriages carried them in comfort over the known world? —the middle classes to whom stage coaches and mails were an accessible mode of conveyance?—or the poor, whom the cost of locomotion condemned often to an almost vegetable existence? Clearly the latter. The railroad is the Magna Carta of their motive freedom. How few among the last generation ever stirred beyond their own village? How few among the present will die without visiting London? . . . The number who left Manchester by cheap trips in one week of holiday time last year exceeded 202,000; against 150,000 in 1849, and 116,000 in 1848.

Institution of Civil Engineers Meeting, January 1856
Chairman and President, Robert Stephenson
Quoted in The Engineer, January 1856

... the president observed that he would apply himself to the great question of British Railways, which were described as spreading, like a network, over Great Britain and Ireland, to the extent of 8,054 miles completed; thus, in length, they exceeded the ten chief rivers of Europe united, and more than enough of single rails were laid to make a belt of iron round the globe. The cost of these lines has been £86,000,000, equal to one third the amount of the national debt. . . . The extent of the railway works was remarkable—they had penetrated the earth with tunnels to the extent of more than fifty miles—there were eleven miles of viaduct in the vicinity of the metropolis alone—the earth-work measure of some 550,000,000 cubic yards—St. Paul's in comparison with the mountain this earth would rear, would be but as a pigmy beside a giant, for it would form a pyramid a mile and a half in height with a base larger than St. James' Park. 80,000,000 train miles were run annually on the railways, 5,000 engines and 150,000 vehicles composed the working stock. The engines, in a straight line, would extend from London to Chatham; the vehicles from London to Aberdeen; and the companies employed 90,400 officers and servants; whilst the engines consumed annually 20,000,000 tons of coal so that in every minute of time four tons of coal flashed into steam twenty tons of water, an amount sufficient for the supply of the domestic and other wants of the town of Liverpool. The coal consumed was equal to the whole amount exported to foreign countries, and to one half of the annual consumption of London. In 1854 111,000,000 passengers were conveyed on the railways, each passenger travelling an average of twelve miles. The old coaches carried an average of ten passengers, and for the conveyance of 300,000 passengers a day 12 miles each, there would have been required at least 10,000 coaches and 120,000 horses. The receipts of the railways in 1854 amounted to £20,215,000 and there was no instance on record in which the receipts of a railway had not been of continuous growth. . . . The wear and tear was great; 20,000 tons of iron required to be replaced annually; and 26,000,000 sleepers annually perished: 300,000 trees were annually felled to make good the loss of sleepers; and 300,000 trees could be grown on little less than 5,000 acres of forest-land. The postal facilities afforded by railways were very great. But for their existence Mr. Rowland Hill's plan could never have been effectually carried out. Railways afforded the means of carrying bulk, which would have been fatal to the old mail coaches. Every Friday night at present, when weekly papers were transmitted, eight or ten vans were now required for Post Office bags on the North Western Railway, and this use of eight or ten railway vans implied, at least, the employment of 14 or 15 mail coaches and the expense of 14 or 15 mail coaches to Birmingham would never have been sustained by a penny postage. For this great blessing, therefore, the nation had to thank the railways. They were the great engines for the diffusion of knowledge. Government could never have carried the 'Times', of its present size, on the same terms, by the old mail coach. The Parliamentary blue books never would have been printed; for except by canal, or by waggon, they could not have been distributed, and if they could not have been circulated they would have been useless.

The results of railways were astounding, 90,000 men were employed directly and upwards of 40,000 collaterally; 130,000 men with their wives and families, representing a population of 500,000 souls; so that one in fifty of the entire population of the kingdom might be said to be dependent on railways. The annual receipt of railways now reaches £20,000,000 or nearly half the amount of the ordinary revenue of the state. If railway intercourse were suspended the same amount of traffic could not be carried on under a cost of £60,000,000 per annum; so that £40,000,000 were saved by the railways. To the public 'time is money' and in point of time, a further saving was effected; for every journey averaging twelve miles in length, an hour was saved to 111,000,000 passengers per annum, which was equal to 38,000 years in the life of a man working eight hours a day, and obtaining an average of 3s. per diem for his work, this additional saving was £2,000,000 a year.'

DOCUMENT 44

R. D. Baxter, Railway Extension and Its Results (1866)
Quoted in Essays in Economic History, Vol 3, ed. Carus-Wilson

Increased facilities of transit led to increased trade; increased trade gave greater employment and improved wages; the diminution in the cost of transit and the repeal of fiscal duties cheapened provisions; and the immense flood of commerce which set in since 1850 has raised the incomes and the prosperity of the working classes to an unprecedented height. Railways were the first cause of this great change and are entitled to share largely with free trade the glory of its subsequent increase and of the national benefit.

Extension of Railways Overseas

DOCUMENT 45

R. D. Baxter, Railway Extension and Its Results (1866), op. cit.

'The Romans were the great road-makers of the ancient world—the English are the great railroad makers of the modern world. The tramway was an English invention, the locomotive was the production of English genius, and the first railways were constructed and carried to success in England. We have covered with railroads the fairest districts of the United Kingdom, and developed railways in our colonies of Canada and India. But we have done much more than this, we have introduced them into almost every civilised country. . . . To this day, wherever an undertaking of more than ordinary difficulty presents itself, the aid is invoked of English engineers, English contractors, English navvies and English shareholders; and a large portion of the rails with which the line is laid, and the engines and rolling stock with which it is worked are brought from England.

Agriculture

Progressive Methods

The improvement of agriculture was a necessary prerequisite for industrialisation, feeding the rising population, providing raw materials like wool, leather, grain and flax, financing investment in transport improvements and releasing labour for new occupations. Norfolk took the lead in agricultural improvement. It was well populated, within reach of the London market by sea and blessed with a light, sandy soil, which made experimentation possible. It must be emphasised, however, that the pace of technical change in agriculture was very slow, despite the propagandist efforts of enthusiasts like Arthur Young.

DOCUMENT 46

A. Young, The Farmer's Tour (1771), Vol 2, letter 14, pp 150, 156, 161

As I shall presently leave Norfolk it will not be improper to give a slight review of the husbandry which has rendered the name of this county so famous in the farming world. Pointing out the practices which have succeeded so nobly here, may perhaps be of some use to other countries possessed of the same advantages, but unknowing in the art to use them.

From forty to fifty years ago, all the northern and western, and a part of the eastern tracts of the county, were sheep walks, let so low as from 6d. to 1s. 6d. and 2s. an acre. Much of it was in this condition only thirty years ago. The great improvements have been made by means of the following circumstances.

First: By inclosing without the assistance of parliament.
Second: By a spirited use of marl and clay.
Third: By the introduction of an excellent course of crops.
Fourth: By the culture of turnips well hand-hoed.
Fifth: By the culture of clover and ray-grass.
Sixth: By landlords granting long leases.
Seventh: By the country being divided chiefly into large farms.

THE COURSE OF CROPS

After the best managed inclosure, and the most spirited in marling, still

47

the whole success of the undertaking depends on this point: No fortune will be made in Norfolk by farming, unless a judicious course of crops be pursued. That which has been chiefly adopted by the Norfolk farmers is,

1. Turnips
2. Barley
3. Clover: or clover and ray-grass
4. Wheat

LARGE FARMS

If the preceding articles are properly reviewed, it will at once be apparent that no small farmers could effect such great things as have been done in Norfolk. Inclosing, marling, and keeping a flock of sheep large enough for folding, belong absolutely and exclusively to great farmers. Nor should it be forgotten that the best husbandry in Norfolk is that of the largest farmers. Great farms have been the soul of the Norfolk culture: split them into tenures of a hundred pounds a year, you will find nothing but beggars and weeds in the whole county.

Advantages of Enclosure

Enclosure was in many cases the necessary preliminary to the adoption of new methods of farming, whether it meant the rationalisation of existing fields or the taking in of common land. Small owners and squatters suffered through their inability to raise the capital for the hedging, ditching and building which accompanied enclosure or because they could produce no written title to land that was customarily theirs. Enclosures made more intensive agriculture possible and thus created rather than diminished employment opportunities. The cause of rural employment in this period was the failure of even the new agriculture to create enough jobs to occupy the rapidly rising and largely immobile rural population.

DOCUMENT 47

John Middleton, View of the Agriculture of Middlesex (1798), pp 106–9
Quoted in M. W. Flinn, Readings in Economic and Social History, pp 82–3

Inclosing.—The benefits and advantages that would be derived from a general inclosure of commons, are so numerous, as far to exceed my powers of description or computation. The opportunity it would afford, of separating dry ground from wet, or well draining the latter, and liming the rotten parts, is of infinite consequence: as such an arrangement would, with the aid of intelligent breeders, be the means of raising a breed of sheep and neat cattle, far superior to the present race of wretched half starved animals now seen in such situations. It would have the effect of supporting a more numerous stock, upon the same quantity of food, by restraining the cattle and sheep within due bounds. Their restless and rambling disposition, not only treads the grass off the ground, but also takes the flesh off their bones. This renders the attendance of a shepherd necessary, and requires likewise that they be driven to and from the fold. Further, the live stock would by this means be rendered many hundreds per cent. more valuable to individuals and the community, than it has hitherto been, or can possibly be, without inclosure: and, *what is of the last, the greatest importance, it would tend to preserve such improved breed from that destructive malady, the rot, which makes such terrible havock among our flocks.* Add to this, that the markets would be more plentifully supplied with beef and mutton, and the price of these articles considerably reduced.

The commons of this kingdom being, with very few exceptions, without ridges, furrows, or drains, have not the means of discharging that superfluous water from the surface of them, which is well known to be of great detriment to vegetation in general. Many commons on low situations, and where the soil happens to be of a retentive quality, hold water like a sponge, which being always stagnant, as well as excessive in quantity, renders the soil of such doubt, the cause of many of the disorders which that animal is subject to, particularly that fatal malady the rot. From the same causes also, the neighbourhood of such commons must be particularly unfriendly to the health and longevity of man. Only let us reverse the scene, and for a moment suppose these commons to be inclosed, the necessary ditches and drains sunk, and the land brought into tillage, and we shall see all the superabundant moisture got rid of; and the water, being kept in constant motion, by trickling down the side of the ridges into the furrows, and from thence, into the ditches and rivulets, will be found to fertilise the very soil which, in its present stagnant state, it serves to injure: while, by leaving the land dry, it will be rendered more healthy both for men and cattle. The effects of such a measure would soon shew themselves in many districts of this island, which, at present, are very unpropitious to the health of man, in the much greater longevity of the inhabitants.

It may farther be observed, that commons are entirely defective in the great article of labour; but no sooner does an inclosure take place, than the scene is agreeably changed from a dreary waste, to the more pleasing one, of the same spot appearing all animation, activity and bustle. Every man, capable of performing such operations, is furnished with plenty of employment, in sinking ditches and drains, in making banks and hedges, and in planting quicks and trees. Nor are the wheelwright, carpenter, smith, and other rural artificers, under the necessity of being idle spectators of the scene, since abundance of work will be found for them, in the erection of farm-houses, and the necessary appendages thereto; and in the forming and making roads, bridges, gates, stiles, implements of husbandry, etc. Even after a few years, when these kind of temporary exertions are over, by the whole being brought into a regular system of husbandry, it will still continue to provide both food and employment for a very increased population.

A Petition Against Enclosure

DOCUMENT 48

Commons Journals, 19th July 1797
Quoted in Bland, Brown and Tawney, English Economic History, p 531

A Petition of the hereunder-signed small Proprietors of Land and Persons entitled to Rights of Common (at Raunds, Northamptonshire).

That the petitioners beg leave to represent to the House that, under the pretence of improving lands in the same parish, the cottagers and other persons entitled to right of common on the lands intended to be enclosed, will be deprived of an inestimable privilege, which they now enjoy, of turning a certain number of their cows, calves, and sheep, on and over the said lands; a privilege that enables them not only to maintain themselves and their families in the depth of winter, when they cannot, even for their money, obtain from the occupiers of other lands the smallest portion of milk or whey for such necessary purpose, but in addition to this, they can now supply the grazier with young or lean stock at a reasonable price, to fatten and bring to market at a more moderate rate for general consumption, which they conceive to be the most rational and effectual way of establishing public plenty and cheapness of provision; and they further conceive, that a more ruinous effect of this enclosure will be the almost total depopulation of their town, now filled with bold and hardy husbandmen, from among whom, and the inhabitants of other open parishes, the nation has hitherto derived its greatest strength and glory, in the supply of fleets and armies, and driving them, from necessity and want of employ, in vast crowds into manufacturing towns, where the very nature of their employment, over the loom or the forge, soon may waste their strength, and consequently debilitate their posterity, and by imperceptible degrees obliterate that great principle of obedience to the Laws of God and their country, which forms the character of the simple and artless villagers, more equally distributed through the open counties, and on which so much depends the good order and government of the state. These are some of the injuries to themselves as individuals, and of the ill consequences to the public, which the petitioners conceive will follow from this, as they have already done from many enclosures, but which they did not think they were entitled to lay before the House (the constitutional patron and protector of the poor) until it unhappily came to their own lot to be exposed to them through the Bill now pending.

DOCUMENT 49

*Marshall's Practical Remarks on Executing the Improvements of Farm
Lands (1804)
Quoted in English Historical Documents, Vol XI*

The first step toward the execution of every improvement is to ascertain its
reality; by calculating the advantages to arise from it, and estimating the
expense of carrying it into effect. . . .

The next point to be ascertained is the practicability, under the given
circumstances of a case, of executing the plan under consideration.

There are three things essential to the due execution of an improvement.
1. An undertaker; or a person of skill, leisure, and activity, to direct the
undertaking. 2. Men and animals with which to prosecute the work. 3.
Money, or other means of answering the required expenditure. A deficiency,
in any one of these, may, by frustrating a well planned work, after its
commencement, be the cause, not only of its failure, but of time, money,
and credit being lost. . . .

By personal attention, only, much is to be done. By reviewing an estate,
once or twice a year;—by conversing with each tenant in looking over his
farm;—and by duly noticing the instances of good management which
rise to the eye, and condemning those which are bad;—vanity and fear,
two powerful stimulants of the human mind, will be roused,— and an emulation be created among superior managers; while shame will scarcely
fail to bring up the more deserving of the inferior ranks. . . .

By encouraging leading men, in different parts of a large estate, men who
are looked up to, by ordinary tenants;—by holding out these as patterns to
the rest;—by furnishing them with the means of improving their breeds
of stock; by supplying them with superior varieties of crops, and with
implements of improved constructions. And, in recluse and backward
districts, much may be done by tempting good husbandmen, and expert
workmen, from districts of a kindred nature, but under a better system of
cultivation, to settle upon an estate.

By an experimental farm, to try new breeds of stock, new crops, new
implements, new operations, and new plans of management: such as ordinary
tenants ought not to attempt,—before they have seen them tried.

Leave it to the professional men, to yeomanry and the higher class of
tenants, to carry on the improvements, and incorporate them with established practices,—to prosecute pecuniary agriculture in a superior manner,—
and set examples to inferior tenantry. This is strictly their province; and
their highest and best view in life. It has been through this order of men,
chiefly or wholly, that valuable improvements in agriculture have been
brought into practice, and rendered of general use.

The possessor of an extent of territory has higher objects to view, and a more elevated station to fill. As a superior member of society, it may be said, he has still higher views than those of aggrandizing his own income. But how can a man of fortune fill what may well be termed his legitimate station in life, with higher advantage to his country, than by promoting the prosperity of his share of its territory; by rendering not one field, or one farm, but every farm upon it, productive? This is, indeed, being faithfully at his post. And it is a good office in society which is the more incumbent upon him, as no other man on earth can of right perform it;—valuable as it is to the public.

The Corn Law of 1815

Corn Laws, that is bounties on the export of grain and prohibitions on its import, date back to the seventeenth century. The prospect of peace and the onset of a series of good harvests in 1813 brought the question of Corn Laws once more into the public area. Agriculturalists (who dominated Parliament) wished to protect investments in new techniques which had been financed by heavy mortgages. Fearing that foreign grain might be imported in quantity they determined to ban its sale until the domestic price of wheat reached 80/- a quarter, the minimum at which they could make a reasonable margin of profit. They also pleaded that the stability and prosperity of agriculture was basic to the welfare of the nation as a whole.

DOCUMENT 50

The Annual Register, Vol 56, p 130

'Without presuming to give any opinion respecting the general justice or policy of the proposed alterations in the system of the Corn Laws, we may venture to observe, respecting the parliamentary proceedings on the subject, 1, that the very high standard fixed in the first set of resolutions for the points at which exportation was to cease, and importation to be allowed, did certainly indicate in the proposers a design of keeping up a price of corn adequate to the support of that extraordinary rise of rents which has taken place of late years: 2, that the great majorities in the House of Commons in favour of the mitigated resolutions cannot in fairness be attributed to any other cause, than a conviction of the public utility of the measures proposed; and 3, that the number of petitions against any change in the existing laws can afford no rule to judge of the merits of the case, when it is considered with what ease a ferment is excited among the people, especially in a matter apparently connected with their subsistence. The question, as a subject of sound and sober policy, cannot be said yet to have received a satisfactory discussion.

Petition Against the 1815 Corn Law

To consumers the Corn Law of 1815 looked like a heartless exploitation of the poor man's need, as bread accounted for about two thirds of a labourer's total expenditure.

DOCUMENT 51

Hansard, vol 30, pp 107–9
Quoted in D. G. Barnes, History of the English Corn Laws, p. 155

To the Honourable the Commons of the United Kingdom of Great Britain and Ireland in Parliament assembled: The Humble Petition of the Inhabitants Householders of the City and Liberties of Westminster, whose names are hereunto subscribed, Sheweth,

That your petitioners, fully sensible of the value of our excellent constitution of government, though always lamenting the limitation and abridgement of its blessings by a corrupt system of administration, and the want of an equal representation of the people, have patiently endured the unexampled burthen of taxation, occasioned by the late protracted, calamitous, and, in their judgment, unnecessary war, although they could not feel that it fell with very unequal severity on the inhabitants of towns, while the owners and occupiers of lands were in general much more than compensated, by the enormous increase of rents, and by the high price of the produce of the earth.

That on the unexpected and fortunate return of peace, it was reasonable to hope, that this forced and unnatural state of things, would be, in a great degree, corrected; that the rent of land and prices of provisions would be reduced; that some of the more grievous and burthensome taxes would cease; that commerce would flow into its accustomed channels; that a stimulus would be given to our manufacturing and trading interests, by the freedom of intercourse with foreign nations; and that all classes of our fellow-subjects would participate in those blessings and advantages to which they had formerly been accustomed in time of tranquility.

That your petitioners have, however, noticed with extreme concern and anxiety the introduction into your honourable House of a Bill relative to the importation of Corn, which, if passed into a law, must necessarily and directly produce, and in the judgment of your petitioners is intended to produce, a great permanent increase in the price of one of the first necessaries of life, for the sake of enabling the proprietors and cultivators of land to maintain undiminished a splendid and luxurious style of living, unknown to their fathers, in which they were tempted to indulge during the late war, so highly profitable to them, and so calamitous to most of their fellow-subjects.

That it appears to your petitioners, that the measure which is the object of this Bill neither has been, nor can be proved to be called for by any necessity; that, on the contrary, the system of prohibition is injudicious, and that whenever the produce of all the land which can be cultivated at a moderate expense, is found insufficient for the support of a greatly increased manufacturing population, it is wiser to import, from countries where it can be grown at a low price, the additional quantity of corn required, which the spirit and industry of our merchants would at all times obtain in exchange for manufactures exported, than to diminish the national capital and increase the price of bread, in attempting to force it from barren spots at home by an enormously expensive mode of cultivation.

That the certain consequences of this prohibitory measure, if persevered in, will be, as your petitioners conceive, considerable inconvenience to the middle orders of society; great distress to the poorer and more numerous classes; a most serious injury to the manufactures and commerce of the country; a great loss of national property; a powerful inducement to emigration; and eventually, though not immediately, a bar to the prosperity of the landed interest itself. For these reasons, they are firmly persuaded that it is both impolitic and unjust.

Your petitioners, therefore, humbly pray that the said Bill may not pass into law, and that the degree of freedom which the corn trade at present enjoys may not be diminished.

And your petitioners shall ever pray.

Depression in Agriculture

The Corn Laws failed to maintain the price of wheat at a level sufficient to guarantee prosperity. Imports were of marginal importance and the real determinant was the weather. In good years the domestic harvest, boosted by newly adopted techniques of production, was too plentiful and demand too inelastic to compensate. In bad years prices rose but there was seldom enough grain available from Europe, which suffered largely the same climate, to alleviate distress. The activities of grain speculators added to the violence of price fluctuations which created an atmosphere of uncertainty, discouraging to new investment.

Speech in the House of Commons by C. C. Western on the distressed state of
agriculture, 7th March 1816
Quoted in English Historical Documents, Vol XI

... Between two and three years ago agriculture was in a flourishing and prosperous state, and yet, within the short period which has since elapsed, thousands have been already ruined, and destruction seems to impend over the property of all those whose capital is engaged in the cultivation of the soil. From what causes, I say, can such events have arisen? Are they the effects of excessive taxation, of the enormous amount of the national debt? Are they the consequences of our extensive paper circulation, which now appears to have been in a great measure withdrawn? Are they occasioned by the pressure of the tithe, or the severe burden of the poor rate? ...

The first and obvious cause, I say, has been a redundant supply in the markets, a supply considerably beyond the demand, and that created chiefly by the produce of our own agriculture. The importation of foreign corn has, no doubt, in some degree, contributed to the creation of that redundance: but as it did not exceed in the last two years the average amount of the last ten, it is evident that the surplus now existing is chiefly ascribable to the extension of our own growth.

Permit me, Sir, here to call to the recollection of the House the effect of a small surplus or deficit of supply above or below the demand of the market. It is perfectly well known that if there is a small deficiency of supply, the price will rise in a ratio far beyond any proportion of such deficiency; the effect indeed is almost incalculable; so likewise on a surplus of supply beyond demand, the price will fall in a ratio exceeding almost tenfold the amount of such surplus. Corn, being an article of prime necessity, is peculiarly liable to such variation; upon a deficit of supply the price is further advanced by alarm; and upon a surplus, it is further diminished by the difficulty the growers have in contracting the amount of their growth, compared to the means which other manufacturers possess of limiting the amount of their manufactures.

... In short, throughout all parts of the Empire, during the last 20 years, agriculture has certainly advanced with rapid strides. The full effect of all our improvements has just been completely realized; and two or three good harvests from this extended and improved agriculture, together with continued import, and demand reduced, have occasioned such a surplus in the market, as very obviously accounts for the first depression of the price.

... though agriculture has advanced rapidly, yet the profits have not been large; and such has been the enterprising spirit of late years, which farmers have evinced equally with all other classes of society, that their earnings have been immediately devoted to further improvements and their capitals have been sunk in the amelioration of their lands, which in a thousand instances will now turn out to have been irrecoverably thrown away. ...

The ruinously low prices of agricultural produce at this moment cannot be ascribed to any deficiency in the protecting power of the law. Protection cannot be carried further than monopoly. This monopoly the British grower has enjoyed for the produce of the two last harvests; the ports (with the exception of the ill-timed and unnecessary importation of oats during six weeks of the last summer) having been uninterruptedly shut against all foreign import for nearly thirty months. . . .

To prohibit the foreign supply altogether, so long as from the casualty of seasons we are subject to years of deficient or damaged produce, has at all times been felt to be impossible. But, since the year 1815 we have had recourse to an absolute prohibition up to a certain price, and an unlimited competition beyond that price.

This system is certainly liable to sudden alterations, of which the effect may be at one time to reduce prices already low, lower than they would probably have been under a state of free trade, and at another, unnecessarily to enhance prices already high; to aggravate the evils of scarcity, and to render more severe the depression of prices from abundance. On the one hand, it deceives the grower with the false hope of a monopoly, and by its occasional interruption, may lead to consequences which deprive him of the benefits of that monopoly, when most wanted; on the other hand, it holds out to the country the prospect of an occasional free trade, but so regulated and desultory as to baffle the calculations and unsettle the transactions, both of the grower and the dealer at home; to deprive the consumer of most of the benefits of such a trade, and to involve the merchant in more than the ordinary risks of mercantile speculation. It exposes the markets of the country, either to be occasionally over-whelmed with an inundation of foreign corn, altogether disproportionate to its wants, or, in the event of any considerable deficiency in our own harvest, it creates a sudden competition on the continent, by the effect of which, the prices there are rapidly and unnecessarily raised against ourselves. . . .

Effects of the Corn Laws

The Corn Laws were revised in 1822 and 1828 but to no effect. In 1838 the Anti-Corn Law League was founded in Manchester, Britain's great export city. It soon enlisted the support of the manufacturing interest by demonstrating that free trade in grain would bring cheap bread, so that employers could push wages down, and by arguing that if Britain bought grain abroad she would thereby generate incomes which could be used to purchase British exports. The public propaganda of the League, however, took a more social and moral line.

E. Elliott, The Black Hole of Calcutta
Quoted in Corn Law Rhymes, pp 70–4

Hopeless trader, answer me!
What hath bread-tax done for thee?
Ask thy lost and owing debts,
Ask our bankrupt-throng'd Gazettes.
Clothier, proud of Peterloo!
Ironmaster, loyal, too!
What hath bread-tax done for you?
Let the Yankee tariff tell,
None to buy, and all to sell;
Useless buildings, castle strong,
Hundred thousands, worth a song;
Starving workmen, warehouse full,
Saxon web, from Polish wool,
Grown where grew the wanted wheat.
Which we might not buy and eat.
Merchants, bread-tax'd trade won't pay,
Profits lessen every day;
Sell thy stock and realize,
Let thy streeted chimneys rise;
And when bread-tax'd ten are two,
Learn what bread-tax'd rents can do.

What hath bread-tax done for me?
Farmer, what for thine and thee?
Ask of those who toil to live,
And the price they cannot give;
Ask our hearths, our gainless marts,
Ask thy children's broken hearts,
Ask their mother, sad and grey,
Destined yet to parish pay.
Bread-tax'd weaver, all can see
What that tax hath done for thee,
And thy children, vilely led,
Singing hymns for shameful bread,
Till the stores of every street,
Know their little naked feet.

Bread-tax-eating absentee,
What hath bread-tax done for thee?—
Cramm'd thee, from our children's plates,
Made thee all that nature hates,

Fill'd thy skin with untaxed wine,
Fill'd thy breast with hellish schemes,
Fill'd thy head with fatal dreams—
Of potatoes, basely sold
At the price of wheat in gold,
And of Britons sty'd to eat
Wheat-priced roots, instead of wheat.

The Growth of Industry

Inventions

The English Genius

The skill of English 'mechanicks' was recognised before the process of industrialisation had begun and was stimulated by the demands of trade and war on the mineral and metallurgical industries.

DOCUMENT 54

J. Tucker, Instructions to Travellers (1757), p 20
Quoted in Charles Wilson, England's Apprenticeship 1603–1763

Few countries are equal, perhaps none excel, the English in the number of contrivances of their Machines to abridge labour. Indeed the Dutch are superior to them in the use and application of Wind Mills for sawing Timber, expressing Oil, making Paper and the like. But in regard to Mines and Metals of all sorts, the English are uncommonly dexterous in their contrivance of the mechanic Powers; some being calculated for landing the Ores out of the Pits, such as Cranes and Horse Engines; others for draining off superfluous Water, such as Water Wheels and Steam Engines; others again for easing the Expense of Carriage such as Machines to run on inclined Planes or Roads downhill with wooden frames, in order to carry many Tons of Material at a Time. And to these must be added the various sorts of Levers used in different processes; also the Brass Battery works, the Slitting Mills, Plate and Flatting Mills, and those for making Wire of different Fineness. Yet all these, curious as they may seem, are little more than Preparations or Introductions for further Operations. Therefore, when we still consider that at Birmingham, Wolverhampton, Sheffield and other manufacturing Places, almost every Master Manufacturer hath a new Invention of his own, and is daily improving on those of others; we may aver with some confidence that those parts of England in which these things are seen exhibit a specimen of practical mechanics scarce to be paralleled in any part of the world.

The Empirical Approach

Most of the significant technical advances of the eighteenth century were made by practical men, rather than academics or theorists. Theory tended to follow practice and set itself to explain natural phenomena which manufacturers knew how to harness but could not explain.

DOCUMENT 55

T. L. Rupp, 'On the Process of Bleaching with the oxygenated muriatic Acid',
Manchester Lit. & Phil. Soc. Memoirs (1798)
Quoted in Musson & Robinson, Science and Technology in the Industrial
Revolution, p 82

The arts (manufactures), which supply the luxuries, conveniences, and necessaries of life, have derived but little advantage from philosophers. . . . In mechanics, for instance, we find that the most important inventions and improvements have been made, not through the reasoning of philosophers, but through the ingenuity of artists (craftsmen), and not unfrequently by common workmen. The chemist, in particular, if we accept the pharmaceutical laboratory, has but little claim on the arts: on the contrary, he is indebted to them for the greatest discoveries and a prodigious number of facts, which form the basis of his science. In the discovery of the art of making bread, of the vinous and acetous fermentations, of tanning, of working ores and metals, of making glass and soap, of the action and applications of manures, and in numberless other discoveries of the highest importance, though they are all chemical processes, the chemist has no share. . . . The art of dyeing has attained a high degree of perfection without the aid of the chemist, who is totally ignorant of the rationale of many of its processes, and the little he knows of this subject is of late date.

The Diffusion of Technology in Great Britain

British entrepreneurs had the stimulus of an expanding market for their goods and a scarcity of *skilled* labour. This gave them the incentive to put into practice developments which would have been of academic interest only in a static economy.

DOCUMENT 56

John Farey to the Select Committee on Patent Laws in 1829
Quoted in Musson & Robinson, Science and Technology in the Industrial
Revolution, p 63

We have derived almost as many good inventions from foreigners, as we have originated among ourselves. The prevailing talent of the English and

Scotch people is to apply new ideas to use, and to bring such applications to perfection, but they do not imagine so much as foreigners; clocks and watches, the coining press, the windmill for draining land, the diving bell, the cylinder paper machine, the stocking frame, figure weaving loom, silk throwsting mill, canal-lock, and turning bridge, the machine for dredging and deepening rivers, the manufacture of alum, glass, the art of dyeing, printing, and the earliest notions of the steam engine, were all of foreign origin; the modern paper-making machine, block machinery, printing machine, and steam boats, the same; there are a multitude of others. . . .

Inevitability of Progress

Inventions were resisted by workers as creators of unemployment but the process of invention acquired its own momentum as control of the actual techniques of production passed from the independent craftsman to the profit-seeking entrepreneur. Inventions released bottlenecks in one part of a production process (e.g. spinning) only to create them elsewhere and necessitate the introduction of further new processes (e.g. the power-loom).

DOCUMENT 57

Samuel Smiles, Industrial Biography (1863), pp 166–7

At a much more recent period new inventions have had to encounter serious rioting and machine-breaking fury. Kay of the fly-shuttle, Hargreaves of the spinning-jenny, and Arkwright of the spinning-frame, all had to fly from Lancashire, glad to escape with their lives. Indeed, says Mr. Bazley, 'so jealous were the people, and also the legislature, of everything calculated to supersede men's labour, that when the Sankey Canal, six miles long, near Warrington, was authorized about the middle of last century, it was on the express condition that the boats plying on it should be drawn by men only!' Even improved agricultural tools and machines have had the same opposition to encounter; and in our own time bands of rural labourers have gone from farm to farm breaking drill-ploughs, winnowing, threshing, and other machines, down even to the common drills,—not perceiving that if their policy had proved successful, and tools could have been effectually destroyed the human race would at once have been reduced to their teeth and nails, and civilisation summarily abolished.

It is, no doubt, natural that the ordinary class of workmen should regard with prejudice, if not with hostility, the introduction of machines calculated to place them at a disadvantage and to interfere with their usual employments; for to poor and not very far-seeing men the loss of daily bread is an appalling prospect. But invention does not stand still on that account. Human brains *will* work. Old tools are improved and new ones invented, superseding existing methods of production, though the weak and unskilled may occasionally be pushed aside or even trodden under foot. The consolation which remains is, that while the few suffer, society as a whole is vastly benefited by the improved methods of production which are suggested, invented, and perfected by the experience of successive generations.

Invention by Perfection

Invention was not a once-for all process. Each manufacturer sought to improve on his rivals, partly to win a competitive advantage, partly to evade the patent laws by making his machines differ slightly from the official specification.

DOCUMENT 58

Samuel Smiles, Industrial Biography (1863), pp. 178–9

It is always difficult to apportion the due share of merit which belongs to mechanical inventors, who are accustomed to work upon each other's hints and suggestions, as well as by their own experience. Some idea of this difficulty may be formed from the fact that, in the course of our investigations as to the origin of the planing machine—one of the most useful of modern tools—we have found that it has been claimed on behalf of six inventors—Fox of Derby, Roberts of Manchester, Matthew Murray of Leeds, Spring of Aberdeen, Clement and George Rennie of London; and there may be other claimants of whom we have not yet heard. But most mechanical inventions are of a very composite character, and are led up to by the labour and the study of a long succession of workers. Thus Savary and Newcomen led up to Watt; Cugnot, Murdock and Trevithick to the Stephensons; and Maudslay to Clement, Roberts, Nasmyth, Whitworth, and many more mechanical inventors. There is scarcely a process in the arts but has in like manner engaged mind after mind in bringing it to perfection.

Steam Power

The Birth of a Partnership

In the fruitful alliance of Boulton and Watt, Matthew Boulton supplied the capital and the commercial vision, James Watt the inventive ability. It was Boulton who induced Watt to persevere with his experiments to perfect the separate condenser and it was Boulton who suggested that Watt create a device to translate reciprocating into rotary motion.

Boulton to Watt, 7th February 1769
Quoted in L. T. C. Rolt, James Watt, pp 47–8

I was excited by two motives to offer you my assistance which were love of you and love of a money-getting, ingenious project. I presumed that your engine would require money, very accurate workmanship and extensive correspondence to make it turn out to the best advantage, and that the best means of keeping up the reputation and doing the invention justice would be to keep the executive part out of the hands of the multitude of empirical engineers, who from ignorance, want of experience and want of necessary convenience, would be very liable to produce bad and inaccurate workmanship; all of which deficiencies would affect the reputation of the invention. To remedy which and produce the most profit, my idea was to settle a manufactory near to my own by the side of our canal where I would erect all the conveniences necessary for the completion of engines, and from which manufactory we would serve all the world with engines of all sizes. By these means and your assistance we could engage and instruct some excellent workmen (with more excellent tools than would be worth any man's while to procure for one single engine) could execute the invention 20 per cent cheaper than it would be otherwise executed, and with as great a difference of accuracy as there is between the blacksmith and the mathematical instrument maker. It would not be worth my while to make for three counties only, but I find it very well worth my while to make for all the world.

The Benefits of Steam-Power

Steam acquired its own prophets and propagandists, who presented its wider application as the first step towards a more perfect world.

Andrew Ure, Philosophy of Manufactures (1835), pp 18–19

The steam-engine is, in fact, the controller general and mainspring of British industry, which urges it onwards at a steady rate, and never suffers it to lag or loiter, till its appointed task be done.

We have already stated that the labour is not incessant in a power-driven factory, just because it is performed in partnership with the workman's never-failing friend, the steam-engine. Those factory employments have been shown to be by far the most irksome and exhausting which dispense with power; so that the way to put the workman comparatively at his ease, is to enlist a steam-engine in his service. Compare the labour of an iron-turner at one of the self-acting lathes so common now in Manchester, and another at one driven by a power-strap as in London, where, however, the cutting-tools are held in the hands and regulated by the power of the arms and dexterity of the fingers. In the former case the mechanism being once adjusted leaves the workman absolutely nothing to do but look on and study the principles of his trade, as the machine will finish its job in a masterly manner, and immediately thereafter come to repose by throwing itself out of gear. From the preceding details, the world may judge of the untruth and even absurdity of much of the pretended evidence scraped together and bespattered on the factories.

Steam-Power and Economic Growth

DOCUMENT 61

A. Ure, The Philosophy of Manufactures (1835), p. 29

There are many engines made by Bolton and Watt, forty years ago, which have continued in constant work all that time with very slight repairs. What a multitude of valuable horses would have been worn out in doing the service of these machines! and what a vast quantity of grain would they have consumed! Had British industry not been aided by Watt's invention it must have gone on with a retarding pace in consequence of the increasing cost of motive power, and would, long ere now, have experienced in the price of horses, and scarcity of waterfalls, an insurmountable barrier to further advancement, could horses, even at the low prices to which their rival, steam, has kept them, be employed to drive a cotton mill at the present day, they would devour all the profits of the manufacturer.

Steam-engines furnish the means not only of their support but of their multiplication. They create a vast demand for fuel; and, while they lend their powerful arms to drain the pits and to raise the coals, they call into employment multitudes of miners, engineers, ship-builders and sailors, and cause the construction of canals and railways; and, while they enable these rich fields of industry to be cultivated to the utmost, they leave thousands of fine arable fields free for the production of food to man, which must otherwise have been allotted to the food of horses. Steam-engines, moreover, by the cheapness and steadiness of their action, fabricate cheap goods, and procure in their exchange a liberal supply of the necessaries and comforts of life, produced in foreign lands.

The Uses of Steam

Steam-power was rapidly adopted in mining, cotton-spinning and to a lesser extent in iron-founding, pottery and brewing. Not until the second third of the nineteenth century did its application become generalised throughout industry, but it had by that time already played a crucial role in stimulating the expansion of key sectors of the economy like coal, iron, cotton and railways.

Steam profoundly changed the speed of communication of goods, persons and news. . . . The effect was to unite the national economy as never before and to make it increasingly sensitive to factors operating on the other side of the world—harvests, wars, changes of government—which could bring prosperity or depression, but which were quite beyond anyone's power to alter or control.

DOCUMENT 62

J. Hassell, A Tour of the Grand Junction Canal (1819), p 62

The first pottery of consequence in this place (Stoke) is Mr. Spode's manufactory of china and earthenware, and is considered one of the most complete establishments of its kind in the kingdom. Some idea may be formed of its extent from the quantity of coal consumed, which is upwards of 200 tons per week, and from the number of ovens wherein the ware is baked, amounting to eighteen large furnaces, many of which are used three times each, weekly, the whole year round. There are about 800 people, of all ages, employed in this concern. The materials used in this manufactory are brought from a considerable distance; the clays from the counties of Dorset, Devon and Cornwall, and the flint principally from Kent. There are two steam engines connected with the manufactory, the oldest of which has been erected nearly forty years, and the other, a most beautiful atmospheric engine of 36 horse power, was put up by Boulton and Watt, about ten years ago. These engines grind all the flints, glazes, colours, etc.; sift the liquid clay, or slip; compress the prepared clay into a more compact mass; and put in motion the throwing wheels and turning lathes, which, in other factories is effected by pedal and manual labour.

DOCUMENT 63

Mechanics Magazine, 1842

'The Great Western fired her signal of arrival in Kingroad (10 miles from Bristol at the mouth of the river) at half past ten on Monday night, in 13 days only from New York. The reporter of the Times went on board, and left her again in an open boat and in a gale of wind before eleven. He reached London by the mail train at half past five. The intelligence was printed and despatched again to Bristol by one of the regular trains, and a copy of the Times was in the cabin of the Great Western, in the roadstead, by 10 o'Clock p.m. These are the wonders of steam navigation, steam travelling, and steam printing.

Textiles

Domestic Textile Production

The pre-existence of a large-scale woollen industry favoured the rapid growth of cotton manufacture, by diffusing the necessary skills and experience throughout the population. The 'domestic' system helped to cushion the transition to full-scale factory production by serving as a reservoir of productive capacity to be tapped in periods of boom demand and shut off in periods of depression. This greatly lightened the cotton-master's burden of fixed capital.

Defoe's Account of the West Riding Cloth Industry

DOCUMENT 64

D. Defoe, A Tour Through the Whole of Great Britain (1724), Vol. 3, pp 144–6

From Blackstone Edge to Halifax is eight miles; and all the way, except from Sowerby to Halifax, is thus up hill and down; so that, I suppose, we mounted up to the clouds, and descended to the water-level, about eight times in that little part of the journey.

But now I must observe to you, that after we passed the second hill, and were come down into the valley again; and so still the nearer we came to Halifax, we found the houses thicker, and the villages greater in every bottom; and not only so, but the sides of the hills, which were very steep every way were spread with houses; for the land being divided into small inclosures, from two acres to six or seven each, seldom more, every three or four pieces of land had an house belonging to them.

In short, after we had mounted the third hill we found the country one continued village, though every way mountainous, hardly an house standing out of a speaking distance from another; and as the day cleared up, we could see at every house a tenter, and on almost every tenter a piece of cloth, kersie, or shalloon; which are the three articles of this country's labour.

Such, it seems, has been the bounty of nature to this county, that two things essential to life, and more particularly to the business followed here, are found in it, and in such a situation as is not to be met with in any part of England, if in the world beside; I mean coals, and running water on the tops of the highest hills. I doubt not but there are both springs and coals lower in these hills; but were they to fetch them thence, it is probable the pits would be too full of water: it is easy, however, to fetch them from the upper parts, the horses going light up, and coming down loaded. This place, then, seems to have been designed by providence for the very purposes to which it is now allotted, for carrying on a manufacture, which can nowhere be so easily supplied with the conveniences necessary for it. Nor is the industry of the people wanting to second these advantages. Though we met few people without doors, yet within we saw the houses full of lusty fellows, some at the dye-vat, some at the loom, others dressing the cloths; the women and children carding, or spinning; all employed from the youngest to the oldest; scarce any thing above four years old, but its hands were sufficient for its own support. Nor a beggar to be seen, nor an idle person, except here and there in an almshouse, built for those that are ancient, and past working. The people in general live long; they enjoy a good air; and under such circumstances hard labour is naturally attended with the blessing of health, if not riches.

The Growth of the Cotton Industry

Cotton was the classic 'growth industry' of the industrial revolution. It was the first industry to be mechanised all the way through though this process was still not complete by 1830, and it pioneered the use of steam-power in manufacture as well as the factory form of production in which extensive division of labour was practised and the machines themselves set the rhythm of production. Cotton created a demand for steam-engines and spinning machinery and thereby stimulated the embryonic engineering industry; the growth of the industry also led to the introduction of the use of chlorine as a bleaching agent. Its demands for fuel were, however, limited; concentrated in and around Lancashire it stimulated investment in transport only indirectly and to a limited extent; its raw material was wholly imported, and most of the finished product was exported; it financed its own growth by the plough-back of profits. Its effects on the rest of the economy were, therefore, limited, and the role that it played in Britain's economic growth was one of exemplar of technical excellence rather than 'leading sector' dragging other industries forward by the weight of its demands for their goods and services. At the peak of its relative importance, and during the period of its most rapid growth, from the 1820s to the 1840s it never accounted for more than 4–4½ per cent of the National Income.

DOCUMENT 65

Edward Baines, History of the Cotton Manufacture in Great Britain (1835)

A cotton-spinning establishment offers a remarkable example of how, by the use of very great power, an enormous quantity of the easiest work can be accomplished. Often we may see in a single building a 100 horse-power steam engine which has the strength of 880 men, set in motion 50,000 spindles besides all the auxiliary machines. The whole requires the service of but 750 workers. But these machines, with the assistance of that mighty power, can produce as much yarn as formerly could hardly have been spun by 200,000 men, so that one man can now produce as much as formerly required 266! Each spindle produces daily from 2½ to 3 hanks of yarn, and thus the 50,000 together will furnish in 12 hours a thread 62,000 English miles in length—that is to say which would encircle the whole earth 2½ times. . . .

At the accession of George III (1760), the manufacture of cotton supported hardly more than 40,000 persons; but since machines have been invented by means of which one worker can produce as much yarn as 200 or 300 persons could at that time, and one person can print as much material as could 100 persons at that time, 1,500,000 or 37 times as many as formerly can now earn their bread from this work. And yet there are still many, even scholars and members of Parliament, who are so ignorant or so blinded by prejudice as to raise a pathetic lament over the increase and spread of the manufacturing system. One would think that the history of cotton manufacture would have made an end to all these Jeremiads long ago, or that they would be heard only occasionally from a few classes of workers to whom, undoubtedly, certain changes may at first, and at least temporarily, bring disadvantage. But there are persons who regard it as a great disaster when they hear that 150,000 persons in our spinning works now produce as much yarn as could hardly be spun with the little hand-wheel by 40,000,000. These people appear to cherish the absurd opinion that if there were no machines, manufacture would really give employment to as many millions as now; nor do they reflect that the whole of Europe would be inadequate for all this work; and that in that case a fifth of the whole population would need to be occupied with cotton-spinning alone! Both experience and reflection

68

teach us just the contrary; and we should certainly maintain that, if we still had to spin with the hand-wheel today, cotton manufacture would employ only a fifth of the present number. That one spinner can now produce as much yarn in a single day as formerly in a year, that fabrics can be bleached in two days to a pure white that would formerly have required six or eight months, is the reason why this industry can provide work and bread to incomparably more persons than formerly; and of such results we should not complain but rather we should greatly rejoice. . . .

Factories

The Factory was a source of wonder and amazement to the tourist, an object of horror to the labouring man, to whom the massive walls resembled nothing so much as the poorhouse or the prison, an impression which factory discipline tended to reinforce.

DOCUMENT 66

Christian P. W. Beuth, Letter to K. F. Schinkel written in 1823
Quoted in F. Klemm, A History of Western Technology

The modern miracles, my friend, are to me the machines here and the buildings that house them, called factories. Such a block is eight or nine stories high, sometimes has 40 windows along its frontage and is often four windows deep. Each floor is twelve feet high, and vaulted along its whole length with arches each having a span of nine feet. The pillars are of iron, as is the girder which they support; the side-walls and the enclosing walls are as thin as cards,—attaining on the second floor a thickness of less than 2 feet 6 inches. It is said that a storm wrecked one such building in that neighbourhood before it had been completed; that may be true, but a hundred of them are now standing unshaken and exactly as they were erected thirty and forty years ago. A number of such blocks stand in very elevated positions which dominate the neighbourhood; and in addition a forest of even taller boiler house chimneys like needles, so that it is hard to imagine how they remain upright; the whole presents from a distance a wonderful spectacle especially at night, when thousands of windows are brilliantly illuminated by gas-light. You can imagine that bright light is necessary, where one worker must watch 840 threads so fine that 260 hanks weight but one pound, and two threads twisted together form the selvedge strand of English lace.

The Fashion for Cotton

Cotton goods found a ready market. At first it was their novelty, later their versatility which impressed. Continued technical progress cut the price of cotton goods until they were within the reach of even the poorest labourer or servant with a few pence to spare.

DOCUMENT 67

Macpherson Annals of Commerce (1805), iv, p 80

Now cotton yarn is cheaper than linen yarn, and cotton goods are very much used in place of cambric, lawns, and other expensive fabrics of flax, and they have almost totally superseded the silks. Women of all ranks, from the highest to the lowest, are clothed in British manufactures of cotton, from the muslin cap on the crown of the head to the cotton stockings under the sole of the foor. . . . With the gentleman cotton stuffs for waistcoats have almost superseded woollen cloths, and silk stuffs, I believe, entirely.

The Cotton Masters

DOCUMENT 68

P. Gaskell, The Manufacturing Population of England (1833), pp 45, 53–4
Quoted in S. Pollard, The Genesis of Modern Management, pp 111–12

The men who did establish themselves were raised by their own efforts—commencing in a very humble way, and pushing their advance by a series of unceasing exertions, having a very limited capital to begin with, or even none at all save that of their own labour . . . the celerity with which some of these individuals accumulated wealth in the early times of steam spinning and weaving are proofs—if any such were wanting—that they were men of quick views, great energy of character, and possessing no small share of sagacity; and were by these means able to avail themselves to the utmost of the golden advantages, which were presented to their grasp, from 1790 to 1817, a time when they supplied the whole universe with the products of manufacture . . . [These] men . . . had a practical acquaintance with machinery, and . . . laboured themselves, assiduously and diligently, [showing] that rapidity of action and quickness of calculation, which were essentially necessary [to] keep pace with the daily improvements projected and carried out around [them].

DOCUMENT 69

Report from the Committee on the State of the Woollen Manufacture of England (1806)

. . . your committee have the satisfaction of seeing, that the apprehensions entertained of factories are not only vicious in principle, but that they are practically erroneous to such a degree that even the very opposite dispositions might be reasonably entertained: nor would it be difficult to prove, that the factories, to a certain extent at least, and in the present day, seem absolutely necessary to the well-being of the domestic system; supplying those very particulars wherein the domestic system must be acknowledged to be inherently defective: for, it is obvious, that the little master manufacturers cannot afford, like the man who possesses considerable capital, to try the experiments which are requisite, and incur the risks, and even losses, which almost always occur, in inventing and perfecting new articles of manufacture, or in carrying to a state of greater perfection articles already established. He cannot learn, by personal inspection, the wants and habits; the arts, manufactures, and improvements of foreign countries; diligence, economy, and prudence are the requisites of his character, not invention, taste, and enterprize; nor would he be warranted in hazarding the loss of any part of his small capital: he walks in a sure road as long as he treads in the beaten track; but he must not deviate into the paths of speculation. The owner of a factory, on the contrary, being commonly possessed of a large capital, and having all his workmen employed under his own immediate superintendance, may make experiments, hazard speculation, invent shorter or better modes of performing old processes, may introduce new articles and improve and perfect old ones, thus giving the range to his taste and fancy, and, thereby alone, enabling our manufacturers to stand the competition with their commercial rivals in other countries. Meanwhile, as is well worthy of remark (and experience abundantly warrants the assertion) many of these new fabrics and inventions, when their success is once established, become general among the whole body of manufacturers: the domestic manufacturers themselves thus benefiting, in the end, from those very factories which had been at first the object of their jealousy. The history of almost all our other manufactures, in which great improvements have been made of late years, in some cases at an immense expense, and after numbers of unsuccessful experiments, strikingly illustrates and enforces the above remarks. It is besides an acknowledged fact, that the owners of factories are often among the most extensive purchasers at the halls, where they buy from the domestic clothier the established articles of manufacture, or are able at once to answer a great and sudden order; while, at home, and under their own superintendance, they make their fancy goods, and any articles of a newer, more costly, or more delicate quality, to which they are enabled by the domestic system to apply a much larger proportion of their capital. Thus, the two systems, instead of rivalling, are mutual aids to each other; each supplying the other's defects, and promoting the other's prosperity. . . .

Linkage Effects

DOCUMENT 70

J. Aiken, A Description of the Country Thirty to Forty Miles around Manchester (1795)
Quoted in Musson and Robinson, Science and Technology in the Industrial Revolution, p 433

The prodigious extension of the several branches of the Manchester (cotton) manufactures had likewise increased the business of several trades and manufactures connected with or dependent upon them. . . . To the iron-mongers shops, which are greatly increased of late, are generally annexed smithies, where many articles are made, even to nails. The tin-plate works have found additional employment in furnishing many articles for spinning machines; as have also the braziers in casting wheels for the motion-work of the rollers used in them; and the clock-makers in cutting them. Harness-makers have been much employed in making bands for carding engines, and large wheels for the first operation of drawing out the cardings, whereby the consumption of strong curried leather has been much increased.

Coal and Iron

The pre-industrial world relied on wood to supply a multiplicity of needs—timber for ships and buildings; fuel for industry and the home; the raw material for furniture, tools, carts and other articles of daily use. By the sixteenth century the shortage of wood was becoming acute in the south-east, the most densely populated area, and the Sussex iron industry was making great inroads on the dwindling supplies of wood for charcoal. Imports of coal to London increased markedly, facilitated by the low cost of coastal transport from Newcastle, where the coal deposits lay within easy reach of the water. Coal which was transported overland sold at double the pithead price at only five miles distance from the mine. Water transport, river, coast or canal, was vital to the development of the coal industry, and incidentally to shipping. Adam Smith estimated that one third of British shipping was engaged in the Newcastle coal trade.

Defoe's Account of the Coal Trade

DOCUMENT 71

D. Defoe, The Complete English Tradesman (1841 Ed.), Vol 2, pp 172-3

The Newcastle coals, brought by sea to London, are bought at the pit, or at the steath or wharf, for under five shillings per chaldron; I suppose I speak with the most; but when they come to London, are not delivered to the consumers under from twenty-five to thirty shillings per chaldron; and when they are a third time loaded on board the lighters in the Thames, and carried through bridge, then loaded a fourth time into the great west country barges, and carried up the river, perhaps to Oxford or Abingdon, and thence loaded a fifth time in carts or waggons, and carried perhaps ten or fifteen, or twenty miles to the last consumer; by this time they are sometimes sold from forty-five to fifty shillings per chaldron; so that the five shillings first cost, including five shillings tax, is increased to five times the prime cost. And because I have mentioned the frequent loading and unloading the coals, it is necessary to explain it here once for all, because it may give a light into the nature of this river and coast commerce, not in this thing only, but in many others; these loadings are thus:—

1. They are dug in the pit a vast depth in the ground, sometimes fifty, sixty, to a hundred fathoms; and being loaded (for so the miners call it) into a great basket or tub, are drawn up by a wheel and horse, or horses, to the top of the shaft, or pit mouth, and there thrown out upon the great heap, to lie ready against the ships come into the port to demand them.

2. They are then loaded again into a great machine called a wagon; which by the means of an artificial road, called a wagon-way, goes with the help of but one horse, and carries two chaldron, or more, at a time, and this, sometimes, three or four miles to the nearest river or water carriage they come at; and there they are either thrown into, or from, a great storehouse, called a steath, made so artificially, with one part close to or hanging over the water, that the lighters or keels can come close to, or under it, and the coals be at once shot out of the wagon into the said lighters, which carry them to the ships, which I call the first loading upon the water.

Tyneside Coalmines, 1829

The 3 million tons of coal raised each year at the beginning of the eighteenth century had tripled by 1800 and by 1830 doubled again,

73

by 1850 this figure had in turn been more than doubled. The steam-engine made it possible to go deeper and deeper shafts meant higher capital outlays. Underground, however, conditions remained primitive; coal was cut and hauled by hand. To the end of the nineteenth century the industry depended on the pick and the shovel and the constant recruitment of a growing army of miners.

Evidence of John Buddle, a famous colliery viewer

DOCUMENT 72

P. P. Report on the state of the Coal Trade, 1829

What is the deepest pit you know?—The deepest pit I am acquainted with as a working pit is 180 fathoms of shaft; but they frequently go deeper by inclined planes under ground.

What is the shallowest?—The shallowest pit that I know of is 23 fathoms and of very inferior coal.

Can you state generally what is the extent of the expense incurred in sinking a single pit?—I have known, in several cases, upwards of £30,000; that includes the machinery requisite for sinking that pit, that is, the steam engine and all its apparatus; that is merely getting to the coal, and it might be called more properly a winning charge than a working charge. . . .

Have you any idea of the capital employed in the coal district?—I should think that the aggregate capital employed by the coal owners on the river Tyne must amount to a million and a half, exclusive of the craft in the river. Some of them are owners of the craft; many of them hire keels or barges. . . .

Have you made any calculation on that vested in collieries on the river Wear?— . . . I should think from 6 to 700,000. . . .

Have you any calculation of the number of men and ships employed on the two rivers . . . ?— . . . The returns from the Tyne are [from] official documents; from the Wear . . . it is by an approximate calculation. The number of persons employed under ground on the Tyne, are, men 4,937, boys 3,554, together 8,491; above ground, men 2,745, boys 718, making 3,463; making the total 11,954, which in round numbers I call 12,000. On the river Wear, I conceive there are 9,000 employed, making 21,000 employed in digging the coal and delivering it to the ships in the two rivers. From the best calculation I have been able to make, it would appear, that averaging the coasting vessels that carry coals to the size of 220 London chaldrons each vessel, there would be 1,400 vessels employed, which would require 15,000 seamen and boys.

Importance of Coal

Coal was fuel for the steam-engines, a major ingredient in the smelting or iron, the basis of the gas industry and an increasingly important source of chemical derivatives. In addition to this it warmed the hearth of every family who could afford it. It made industrialisation possible by providing an enormous and previously untouched reservior of potential power and heat, removing a crucial bottleneck in the whole process of industrial growth.

DOCUMENT 73

B. Faujas de St. Fond, A Journey Through England and Scotland to the Hebrides in 1784, pp 346–9

From the activity of its manufactures and its commerce, Birmingham is one of the most curious towns in England. If any one should wish to see in one comprehensive view, the most numerous and most varied industries ... it is hither that he must come. ... I say with pleasure, and it cannot be too often said to Frenchmen, that it is the abundance of coal which has performed this miracle and has created, in the midst of a barren desert, a town with forty thousand inhabitants, who live in comfort, and enjoy all the conveniences of life.

An Ironworks

Iron was the basic material of industrialisation. Cheap and durable, it provided bridges, cannon, anchors, lock gates, roof members and rails as well as steam-engines and machinery, and a whole range of household goods for domestic and export sale.

DOCUMENT 74

A. Young, A Six Months' Tour through the North of England (1770), Vol III, pp 10–15

About five miles from Newcastle are the ironworks, late Crowley's, supposed to be the greatest manufactory of the kind in Europe. Several hundred hands are employed in it, insomuch that £20,000 a year is paid in wages. They earn from 1s. to 2d. 6d. a day: and some of the foremen so high as £200 a year. The quantity of iron they work is very great, employing three ships to the Baltic, that each make ten voyages yearly, and bring seventy tons at a time, which amounts to 2,100 tons, besides 500 tons more freighted in others. They use a good deal of American iron, which is as good as any Swedish, and for some purposes much better. . . .

They manufacture anchors as high as 70 cwt., carriages of cannon, hoes, spades, axes, hooks, chains, etc., etc. In general their greatest work is for exportation, and are employed very considerably by the East India Company. They have of late had a prodigious artillery demand from that Company. During the war their business was extremely great: it was worse upon the peace; but for anchors and mooring chains the demand these last seven or eight years has been very regular and spirited. Their business in general, for some time past, has not been equal to what it was in the war. As to the machines for accelerating several operations in the manufacture, the copper rollers for squeezing bars into hoops, and the scissors for cutting bars of iron, the turning cranes for moving anchors into and out of the fire, the beating hammer lifted by the cogs of a wheel; these are machines of manifest utility, simple in their construction, and all moved by water. But I cannot conceive the necessity of their executing so much of the remaining work by manual labour. I observed eight stout fellows hammering an anchor in spots which might evidently be struck by a hammer or hammers moved by water, upon a vast anvil, the anchor to be moved with the utmost ease and quickness, to vary the seat of the strokes.

Henry Cort—His Manufacture of Bar-Iron

DOCUMENT 75

Samuel Smiles, Industrial Biography (1863), pp 119–20

The processes described by Cort in his two patents have been followed by iron manufacturers, with various modifications, the results of enlarged experience, down to the present time. After the lapse of seventy-eight years, the language employed by Cort continues on the whole a faithful description of the processes still practised: the same methods of manufacturing bar from cast-iron, and of puddling, piling, welding, and working the bar-iron, through grooved rollers—all are nearly identical with the methods of manufacture perfected by Henry Cort in 1784. It may be mentioned that the development of the powers of the steam-engine by Watt had an extraordinary effect upon the production of iron. It created a largely increased demand for the article for the purposes of the shafting and machinery which it was employed to drive; while at the same time it cleared pits of water which before were unworkable, and by being extensively applied to the blowing of iron-furnaces and the working of the rolling-mills, it thus gave a still further impetus to the manufacture of the metal. It would be beside our purpose to enter into statistical detail on the subject; but it will be sufficient to state that the production of iron, which in the early part of last century amounted to little more than 12,000 tons, about the middle of the century to about 18,000 tons, and at the time of Cort's inventions to about 90,000 tons, was found, in 1820, to have increased to 400,000 tons; and now the total quantity produced is upwards of four millions of tons of pig-iron every year, or more than the entire production of all other European countries. There is little reason to doubt that this extraordinary development of the iron manufacture has been in a great measure due to the inventions of Henry Cort. It is said that at the present time there are not fewer than 8,200 of Cort's furnaces in operation in Great Britain alone.

Neilson's Hot Blast

DOCUMENT 76

Samuel Smiles, Industrial Biography (1863), pp 159–61

The invention of the hot blast, in conjunction with the discovery of the Black Band ironstone, has had an extraordinary effect upon the development of the iron-manufacture of Scotland. The coals of that country are generally unfit for coking, and lose as much as 55 per cent. in the process. But by using the hot blast, the coal could be sent to the blast-furnace in its raw state, by which a large saving of fuel was effected. Even coals of an inferior quality were by its means made available for the manufacture of iron. But one of the peculiar qualities of the Black Band ironstone is that in many cases it contains sufficient coaly matter for purposes of calcination, without any admixture of coal whatever. Before its discovery, all the iron manufactured in Scotland was made from clay-band; but the use of the latter has in a great measure been discontinued wherever a sufficient supply of Black Band can be obtained. And it is found to exist very extensively in most of the midland Scotch counties,—the coal and iron measures stretching in a broad belt from the Firth of Forth to the Irish Channel at the Firth of Clyde. At the time when the hot blast was invented, the fortunes of many of the older works were at a low ebb, and several of them had been discontinued but they were speedily brought to life again wherever Black Band could be found. In 1829, the year after Neilson's patent was taken out, the total make of Scotland was 29,000 tons. As fresh discoveries of the mineral were made, in Ayrshire and Lanarkshire, new works were erected, until, in 1845, we find the production of Scotch pig-iron had increased to 475,000 tons. It has since increased to upwards of a million of tons, nineteen-twentieths of which are made from Black Band ironstone.

Employment has thus been given to vast numbers of our industrial population, and the wealth and resources of the Scotch iron districts have been increased to an extraordinary extent. During the last year there were 125 furnaces in blast throughout Scotland, each employing about 400 men in making an average of 200 tons a week; and the money distributed amongst the workmen may readily be computed from the fact that, under the most favourable circumstances, the cost of making iron in wages alone amounts to 36s. a ton.

Growth of the Industry

DOCUMENT 77

W. Pitt, General View of the Agriculture of the county of Stafford (1794), p 165
Quoted in English Historical Documents, Vol XI

The extent of the iron trade in all its varieties, wrought and unwrought, for agricultural and other internal purposes, and for home consumption and exportation, under its innumerable shapes and forms, is now so very great, as to rival even that of the great staple, wool; and to make the superiority of the latter somewhat questionable; and from the abundance of iron ore and fuel with which this country abounds, the trade, particularly so far as relates to the production of the metal, is capable of being much extended. . . .

Iron for Machinery

DOCUMENT 78

A. and F. de La Rochefoucauld-Liancourt, Voyage aux Montagnes, Letter dated 9.5.1786
Quoted in P. Mantoux, Industrial Revolution in C18, p 310

I here admired [in a Paisley cotton mill], as in all the large factories I have had the chance of seeing in England, their skill in working iron and the great advantage it gives them as regards the motion, lastingness and accuracy of machinery. All driving wheels, and in fact almost all things, are made of cast iron, of such a fine and hard quality that when rubbed it polishes up just like steel . . . There is no doubt but that the working of iron is one of the most essential of trades and the one in which we are the most deficient. It is the only way by which we can manufacture on a large scale and qualify ourselves to compete on equal terms with the English. For it is impossible for, say, our spinning mills, to attempt to compete with those machines, and for our wooden machinery to try to rival that made of iron.

DOCUMENT 79

Baron Dupin, The Commercial Power of Great Britain (1825), Vol 2,
p 279
Quoted in Clapham, An Economic History of Modern Britain, Vol I, p 6

The more recent the construction of the maritime works of Liverpool is, the less wood is found in their composition . . . the capstans, the rollers . . . the footways across the gates of the locks, the railings along the side of these footways etc; all these things are . . . in constructions of a more modern date, entirely of iron. . . . This is not the effect of any particular whim, or of a short-lived fashion; it is the necessary result of a comparison between the small cost of this material and the high price of wood.

Engineering

The Engineers of the Eighteenth Century

The engineering industries were both the basis and the product of the mechanisation of manufacture. Their role was fundamental, but has attracted strangely little attention from economic historians and interest has only recently been revived by the growth of the study of industrial archaeology and by increasing interest in the history of technology itself. This new emphasis has not as yet made any great impact on economic history below university level, and therefore it seems particularly appropriate that this collection of documents should include a section on 'Engineering'. One of the major difficulties for the historian is to decide what 'engineering' actually means and in the past its component aspects have been split up and studied under separate headings—railways, canals, steam power, shipping, etc. The following selection of documents attempts to illustrate some of the features of the engineering industries which played such an important role in promoting Britain's industrialisation.

DOCUMENT 80

Campbell London Tradesmen (1747), Appendix, p 323
Quoted in W. H. G. Armytage, A Social History of Engineering

The Engineer makes Engines for raising of Water by Fire, either for supplying Reservoirs or draining Mines. . . . The Engineer requires a very mechanically turned head. . . . He employs Smiths of various sorts, Founders for his Brass work, Plumbers for his Leadwork, and a Class of Shoe-makers for making his Leather Pipes. He requires a large stock (at least £500, it is said elsewhere) to set up with, and a considerable Acquaintance among the Gentry. . . . He ought to have a solid, not a flighty Head, otherwise his Business will tempt him to many useless and expensive Projects. The Workmen . . . earn from Fifteen to Twenty Shillings a week; and the Fore man of a Shop, who understands the finishing of the common Engines, may earn much more.

The Millwrights

DOCUMENT 81

William Fairbairn, Treatise on Mills and Mill-work (1861), Vol 1, p 6

The millwright of former days was to a great extent the sole representative of mechanical art, and was looked upon as the authority in all the applications of wind and water, under whatever conditions they were to be used, as a motive power for the purposes of manufacture. He was the engineer of the district in which he lived, a kind of jack-of-all-trades who could with equal facility work at the lathe, the anvil, or the carpenter's bench. In country districts, far removed from towns, he had to exercise all these professions, and he thus gained the character of an ingenious, roving, rollicking blade, able to turn his hand to anything, and, like other wandering tribes in days of old, went about the country from mill to mill, with the old song of 'kettles to mend' reapplied to the more important fractures of machinery.

Thus the millwright of the last century was an itinerant engineer and mechanic of high reputation. He could handle the axe, the hammer, and the plane with equal skill and precision: he could turn, bore, or forge with ease and despatch of one brought up to these trades, and he could set out and cut in the furrows of a millstone with an accuracy equal or superior to that of the miller himself. These various duties he was called upon to exercise, and seldom in vain, as in the practice of his profession he had mainly to depend upon his own resources. Generally, he was a fair arithmetician, knew something of geometry, levelling, and mensuration, and in some cases possessed a very competent knowledge of practical mathematics. He could calculate the velocities, strength, and power of machines; could draw in plan and section, and could construct buildings, conduits, or watercourses, in all the forms and under all the conditions required in his professional practice; he could build bridges, cut canals, and perform a variety of work now done by civil engineers. Such was the character and condition of the men who designed and carried out most of the mechanical work of this country, up to the middle and end of the last century. Living in a more primitive state of society than ourselves, there probably never existed a more useful and independent class of men than the country millwrights. The whole mechanical knowledge of the country was centred amongst them.

Division of Labour—Watches

DOCUMENT 82

A General Description of All Trades (1747)
Quoted in M. D. George, London Life in the Eighteenth Century (1925)

The work of watchmaking [has been brought] to such an exactiness that no hand can imitate it. The movement-maker forges his wheels and turns them to the just dimensions, sends them to the cutter, and has them cut at a trifling expense. He has nothing to do when he takes them from the cutter but to finish them and turn the corners of the teeth. The pinions made of steel are drawn at the mill so that the watchmaker has only to file down the points and fix them to the proper wheels. The springs are made by a trades-man who does nothing else, and the chains by another. These last are frequently made by women. . . . There are workmen who make nothing else but the caps and studs for watches. The watchmaker puts his name on the plate and is esteemed the maker, though he has not made in his shop the smallest wheel belonging to it.

Scarcity of Machinery

DOCUMENT 83

Samuel Smiles, Industrial Biography (1863), pp 211–12

. . . WHEN Sir Samuel Bentham made a tour through the manufacturing districts of England in 1791, he was surprised to find how little had been done to substitute the invariable accuracy of machinery for the uncertain dexterity of the human hand. Steam-power was as yet only employed in driving spinning-machines, rolling metals, pumping water, and such like purposes. In the working of wood no machinery had been introduced beyond the common turning-lathe and some saws, and a few boring tools used in making blocks for the navy. Even saws worked by inanimate force for slitting timber, though in extensive use in foreign countries, were nowhere to be found in Great Britain. As everything depended on the dexterity of hand and correctness of eye of the workmen, the work turned out was of very unequal merit, besides being exceedingly costly. Even in the construc-tion of comparatively simple machines, the expense was so great as to present a formidable obstacle to their introduction and extensive use; and but for the invention of machine-making tools, the use of the steam-engine in the various forms in which it is now applied for the production of power could never have become general.

Joseph Bramah

DOCUMENT 84

Samuel Smiles, Industrial Biography (1863), p 193–4

Bramah's inventive genius displayed itself alike in small things as in great— in a tap wherewith to draw a glass of beer, and in a hydraulic machine capable of tearing up a tree by the roots. His powers of contrivance seemed inexhaustible, and were exercised on the most various subjects. When any difficulty occurred which mechanical ingenuity was calculated to remove, recourse was usually had to Bramah, and he was rarely found at a loss for a contrivance to overcome it. Thus, when applied to by the Bank of England in 1806, to construct a machine for more accurately and expeditiously printing the numbers and date lines on Bank notes, he at once proceeded to invent the requisite model, which he completed in the course of a month. He subsequently brought it to great perfection—the figures in numerical succession being changed by the action of the machine itself,—and it still continues in regular use. Its employment in the Bank of England alone saved the labour of a hundred clerks; but its chief value consisted in its greater accuracy, the perfect legibility of the figures printed by it, and the greatly improved check which it afforded.

Henry Maudslay—Principle of the Slide Rest

DOCUMENT 85

Samuel Smiles, Industrial Biography (1863), pp 213–14

The effects of the introduction of the slide rest were very shortly felt in all departments of mechanism. Though it had to encounter some of the ridicule with which new methods of working are usually received, and for a time was spoken of in derision as 'Maudslay's Go-cart,'—its practical advantages were so decided that it gradually made its way, and became an established tool in all the best mechanical workshops. It was found alike capable of executing the most delicate and the most ponderous pieces of machinery; and as slide-lathes could be manufactured to any extent, machinery, steam-engines, and all kinds of metal work could now be turned out in a quantity and at a price that, but for its use, could never have been practicable. In course of time various modifications of the machine were introduced—such as the planing machine, the wheel-cutting machine, and other beautiful tools on the slide-rest principle,—the result of which has been that extra-ordinary development of mechanical production and power which is so characteristic a feature of the age we live in.

The Growth of Mass-Production Engineering

DOCUMENT 86

Love and Barton, Manchester As It Is (1839), pp 213–19
Quoted in Musson and Robinson, Science and Technology in the Industrial Revolution, p 495

With a view to secure the greatest amount of convenience for the removal of heavy machinery from one department to another, the entire establishment had been laid out with this object in view; and in order to attain it, what may be called the straight line system has been adopted, that is, the various workshops are all in a line, and so placed, that the greater part of the work, as it passes from one end of the foundry to the other, receives in succession, each operation which ought to follow the preceding one, so that little carrying backward and forward, or lifting up and down, is required. . . . By means of a railroad, laid through as well as all round the shops, any casting, however ponderous or massy, may be removed with the greatest care, rapidity, and security.

The whole of this establishment is divided into departments, over each of which a foreman, or responsible person, is placed, whose duty is not only to see that the men under his superintendence produce good work, but also to endeavour to keep pace with the productive powers of all the other departments. The departments may be thus specified:—The drawing office, where the designs are made out; and the working drawings produced. . . . Then come the pattern-makers . . . next comes the Foundry, and the iron and brass moulders; then the forgers or smiths. The chief part of the produce of the last named pass on to the turners and planers. . . . Then comes the fitters and filers . . . in conjunction with this department is a class of men called erectors, that is, men who put together the framework, and the larger part of most machines, so that the last two departments . . . bring together and give the last touches to the objects produced by all the others.

Diffusion of Skills

DOCUMENT 87

Samuel Smiles, Industrial Biography (1863), pp 232–3

The vigilant, the critical, and yet withal the generous eye of the master-being over all his workmen, it will readily be understood how Maudslay's work came to be regarded as a first-class school for mechanical engineers. Every one felt that the quality of his workmanship was fully understood; and, if he had the right stuff in him, and was determined to advance, that his progress in skill would be thoroughly appreciated. It is scarcely necessary to point out how this feeling, pervading the establishment, must have operated, not only in maintaining the quality of the work, but in improving the character of the workmen. The results were felt in the increased practical ability of a large number of artisans, some of whom subsequently rose to highest distinction. Indeed it may be said that what Oxford and Cambridge are in letters, workshops such as Maudslay's and Penn's are in mechanics. Nor can Oxford and Cambridge men be prouder of the connection with their respective colleges than mechanics such as Whitworth, Nasmyth, Roberts, Muir, and Lewis, are of their connection with the school of Maudslay for all these distinguished engineers at one time or another formed part of his working staff, and were trained to the exercise of their special abilities under his own eye. The result has been a development of mechanical ability the like of which perhaps is not to be found in any age or country.

James Nasmyth—Steam Hammer

DOCUMENT 88

Samuel Smiles, Industrial Biography (1863), p 288–9

The first hammer, of 30 cwt., was made for the Patricroft works, with the consent of the partners; and in the course of a few weeks it was in full work. The precision and beauty of its action—the perfect ease with which it was managed, and the untiring force of its percussive blows—were the admiration of all who saw it; and from that moment the steam-hammer became a recognised power in modern mechanics. The variety or gradation of its blows was such, that it was found practicable to manipulate a hammer of ten tons as easily as if it had only been of ten ounces weight. It was under such complete control that while descending with its greatest momentum, it could be arrested at any point with even greater ease than any instrument used by hand. While capable of forging an Armstrong hundred-pounder, or the sheet-anchor for a ship of the line, it could hammer a nail, or crack a nut without bruising the kernel. When it came into general use, the facilities which it afforded for executing all kinds of forging had the effect of greatly increasing the quantity of work done, at the same time that expense was saved. The cost of making anchors was reduced by at least 50 per cent., while the quality of the forging was improved. Before its invention the manufacture of a shaft of 15 or 20 cwt. required the concentrated exertions of a large establishment, and its successful execution was regarded as a great triumph of skill: whereas forgings of 20 and 30 tons weight are now things of almost every-day occurrence. Its advantages were so obvious that its adoption soon became general, and in the course of a few years Nasmyth steam-hammers were to be found in every well-appointed workshop both at home and abroad.

James Nasmyth—His Pile Driver

DOCUMENT 89

Samuel Smiles, Industrial Biography (1863), p 291

Mr. Nasmyth subsequently applied the principle of the steam-hammer in the pile driver, which he invented in 1845.

. . . In forming coffer-dams for the piers and abutments of bridges, quays, and harbours, and in piling the foundations of all kinds of masonry, the steam pile driver was found of invaluable use by the engineer. At the first experiment made with the machine, Mr. Nasmyth drove a 14 inch pile fifteen feet into hard ground at the rate of 65 blows a minute. The driver was first used in forming the great steam dock at Devonport, where the results were very striking; and it was shortly after employed by Robert Stephenson in piling the foundations of the great High Level Bridge at Newcastle, and the Border Bridge at Berwick, as well as in several other of his great works. The saving of time effected by this machine was very remarkable, the ratio being as 1 to 1,800; that is, a pile could be driven in four minutes that before required twelve hours.

Whitworth and Accuracy

DOCUMENT 90

Samuel Smiles, Industrial Biography (1863), pp 273-4

. . . The minute accuracy of Mr. Whitworth's machines is not the least of their merits; and nothing will satisfy him short of perfect truth. At the meeting of the Institute of Mechanical Engineers at Glasgow in 1856 he read a paper on the essential importance of possessing a true plane as a standard of reference in mechanical constructions, and he described elaborately the true method of securing it,—namely, by scraping, instead of by the ordinary process of grinding. At the same meeting he exhibited a machine of his invention by which he stated that a difference of *the millionth part* of an inch in length could at once be detected. He also there urged his favourite idea of uniformity, and proper gradations of size of parts, in all the various branches of the mechanical arts, as a chief means towards economy of production—a principle, as he showed, capable of very extensive application. To show the progress of tools and machinery in his own time, Mr. Whitworth cited the fact that thirty years since the cost of labour for making a surface of cast-iron true—one of the most important operations in mechanics—by chipping and filing by the hand, was 12s. a square foot; whereas it is now done by the planing machine at a cost for labour of less than a a penny. Then in machinery, pieces of 74 reed printing-cotton cloth of 29 yards each could not be produced at less cost than 30s. 6d. per piece; whereas the same description is now sold for 3s. 9d.

Progress of the Industry

DOCUMENT 91

Wm. Fairbairn, Presidential Address to British Association at Manchester, 1861
Quoted in L. T. C. Rolt, Tools for the Job, p 91

When I first entered this city (1814) the whole of the machinery was executed by hand. There were neither planing, slotting nor shaping machines; and, with the exception of very imperfect lathes and a few drills, the preparatory operations of construction were effected entirely by the hands of the workmen. Now, everything is done by machine tools with a degree of accuracy which the unaided hand could never accomplish. The automaton or self-acting machine tool has within itself an almost creative power; in fact, so great are its powers of adaptation that there is no operation of the human hand that it does not imitate.

Part 2

THE SOCIAL IMPACT

The Labour Force

Preface

Britain's economic expansion in the late eighteenth and early nineteenth centuries was achieved by the sum total of the self-interested decisions of the thousands of farmers, manufacturers and merchants who controlled the resources of the nation—the land and its mineral wealth, the labour force, its skills and energy. Their decisions allocated resources to new points of growth within the economy and the consequences of their decisions were not only economic but social. New occupations were created and new skills required; even more rapidly old skills were eliminated and old crafts destroyed. A new labour force was created to serve the needs of new industries employing new techniques of production and enforcing a new discipline in which the hours of labour followed the rhythm of steam rather than the rhythms of Nature. For hundreds of thousands of men, women and children these changes brought new opportunities and new aspirations, balanced by new modes of exploitation and new depths of misery. It is important to remember that the factory worker was still untypical in 1851, that agriculture still employed more labour than any other single occupation and that twice as many people were employed in domestic service as in cotton manufacture, a ratio which was to increase in the second half of the century. It is important also to realise that many occupations were not transformed by machinery, particularly building, and that the small, labour-intensive unit of production, where a dozen men and boys made boots or furniture, remained 'typical' until well into the second half of the nineteenth century.

Factory Labour

Recruitment of Labour

DOCUMENT 92

N. Senior, Grounds and Objects of the Budget, p 506
Quoted in Coats, 'The Classical Economists and the Labourer' in 'Land,
Labour and Population in the Industrial Revolution,' ed Jones & Mingay,
p 119

A girl of 18 can attend to a power-loom as well as a full-grown man; a child of 13 is more valuable as a piecer than an adult—its touch is more sensitive, and its sight is more acute. A factory lad of 18 who marries a factory girl of the same age, finds himself immediately richer; and although he may be pinched during some of the following years, yet as each child attains the age of 9 years it can earn more than its support; and the earnings of 3 children between the ages of 9 and 16 can, in prosperous times, support the whole family. It was under the influence of this enormous stimulus, with some assistance from immigration, that the population of our manufacturing districts increased during the thirty years that elapsed between 1801 and 1831 . . . at a rate equalled only in some portions of America.

DOCUMENT 93

Evidence given by an inhabitant of Bolton before the Factory Commission
of 1834 (Supplementary Report, I), p 169
W. Bowden, Industrial Society in England towards the end of the Eighteenth
Century, p 97

You have been a witness of growth of the operative class in these parts; you have seen it grow from nothing into a great body in the space of a few years. How was it recruited? Of what was it composed? What were the spinners taken from?

A good many from agricultural parts; a many from Wales; a many from Ireland and from Scotland. People left other occupations and came to spinning for the sake of the high wages. I recollect shoemakers leaving their employ and learning to spin. I recollect tailors, I recollect colliers, but a great many more husbandmen left their employ to learn to spin. . . .

Factory Conditions

William Cobbett, Radical politician and journalist, was a virulent opponent of the factory system, as a glance at the following passage will show. In his yearning for a return to the agrarian England of the eighteenth century he was less than fair in his criticisms, but his vitriolic invective does highlight some of the worst excesses committed in the pursuit of profit.

DOCUMENT 94

William Cobbett, Political Register, 20th November 1824, Vol II

Some of these lords of the loom have in their employ thousands of miserable creatures. In the cotton-spinning work these creatures are kept, fourteen hours in each day, locked up, summer and winter, in a heat of from EIGHTY TO EIGHTY-FOUR DEGREES. The rules which they are subjected to are such as no negroes were ever subjected to. I once before noticed a statement made on the part of these poor creatures, relative to their treatment in the factories of Lancashire. This statement is dated on 15th of February 1823, and was published at Manchester by J. Phenix, No 12 Bow Street, in that blood-stained town. This statement says that the heat of the factories is from eighty to eighty-four degrees. A base agent of the Cotton Lords, who publishes a newspaper at Stockport, has lately accused me of exaggeration in having stated the heat at eighty-four degrees.

Now, the statement of which I am speaking was published at Manchester; and does any man believe that such a statement would have been published there if it had not been founded on fact? There was a controversy going on at the time of the publishing of this statement. I read very carefully the answer to this statement; but this answer contained no denial of the heat being from eighty to eighty-four degrees.

Now, then, do you duly consider what a heat of eighty-two is? Very seldom do we feel such a heat as this in England. The 31st of last August, and the 1st, 2nd, and 3rd of last September, were very hot days. The newspapers told us that men had dropped down dead in the harvest fields and that many horses had fallen dead upon the road; and yet the heat during those days never exceeded eighty-four degrees in the hottest part of the day. We were retreating to the coolest rooms in our houses; we were pulling off our coats, wiping the sweat off our faces, puffing, blowing, and panting; and yet we were living in a heat nothing like eighty degrees. What, then, must be the situation of the poor creatures who are doomed to toil, day after day, for three hundred and thirteen days in the year, fourteen hours in each day, in an average heat of eighty-two degrees? Can any man, with a heart in his body, and a tongue in his head, refrain from cursing a system that produces such slavery and such cruelty?

Observe, too, that these poor creatures have no cool room to retreat to, not a moment to wipe off the sweat, and not a breath of air to come and interpose itself between them and infection. The 'door of the place wherein they work, is *locked*, except *half an hour*, at tea-time; the workpeople are not allowed to send for water to drink, in the hot factory; even the *rain-water is locked up*, by the master's order, otherwise they would be happy to drink even that. If any spinner be found with his *window open*, he is to pay a fine of a shilling'! Mr. Martin of Galway has procured Acts of Parliament to be passed to prevent *cruelty to animals*. If horses or dogs were shut up in a place like this they would certainly be thought worthy of Mr. Martin's attention.

Not only is there not a breath of sweet air in these truly infernal scenes; but, for a large part of the time, there is the abominable and pernicious stink of the GAS to assist in the murderous effects of the heat. In addition to the heat and the gas; in addition to the noxious effluvia of the gas, mixed with the steam, there are the *dust*, and what is called the *cotton-flyings* or *fuz*, which the unfortunate creatures have to inhale; and the fact is, the notorious fact is, that well-constituted men are rendered old and past labour at forty years of age, and that children are rendered decrepit and deformed, and thousands upon thousands of them slaughtered by consumptions, before they arrive at the age of sixteen. And are these establishments to boast of? If we were to admit the fact they compose an addition to the population of the country; if we were further to admit that they caused an addition to the pecuniary resources of the Government, ought not a government to be ashamed to derive resources from such means?

If we wanted any proof of the *abject slavery* of these poor creatures, what proof do we want more than the following list of fines?

Any Spinner found with his window open	1s.
Any Spinner found washing himself	1s.
Any Spinner leaving his oil-can out of its place	6d.
Any Spinner putting his gas out too soon	1s.
Any Spinner spinning with his gas-light too long in the morning	2s.
Any Spinner *heard whistling*	1s.
Any Spinner being five minutes after the last bell rings	2s.
Any Spinner being sick and cannot find another Spinner to give satisfaction, to *pay for steam*, per day	6d.

Factory Time

DOCUMENT 95

Evidence of R. Cookson, a hosier, before the Committee on the Woollen Manufacture of England in Parliamentary Papers (1806)

I found the utmost distaste on the part of the men, to any regular hours or regular habits. . . . The men themselves were considerably dissatisfied, because they could not go in and out as they pleased, and have what holidays they pleased, and go on just as they had been used to do; and were subject, during after-hours, to the ill-natured observations of other workmen, to such an extent as completely to disgust them with the whole system. . . .

Discipline in Marshall's Flax Mill

DOCUMENT 96

Rimmer, Marshalls, p 119
Quoted in S. Pollard, Genesis of Modern Management, p 216

So strict are the instructions that if an overseer of a room be found talking to any person in the mill during working hours he is dismissed immediately —two or more overseers are employed in each room, if one be found a yard out of his ground he is discharged . . . everyone, manager, overseers, mechanics, oilers, spreaders, spinners and reelers, have their particular duty pointed out to them, and if they transgress, they are instantly turned off as unfit for their situation.

The Daily Round

DOCUMENT 97

P. Gaskell, The Manufacturing Population of England, Ch. 4

The mode of life which the system of labour pursued in manufactories forces upon the operative, is one singularly unfavourable to domesticity.

Rising at or before day-break, between four and five o'clock the year round, scarcely refreshed by his night's repose, he swallows a hasty meal, or hurries to the mill without taking any food whatever. At eight o'clock half an hour, and in some instances forty minutes, are allowed for breakfast. In many cases, the engine continues at work during mealtime, obliging the labourer to eat and still overlook his work. This, however, is not universal. This meal is brought to the mill, and generally consists of weak tea, of course nearly cold, with a little bread; in other instances, of milk-and-meal porridge. Tea, however, may be called the universal breakfast, flavoured of late years too often with gin or other stimulants.

Where the hands live in immediate proximity to the mill, they visit home; but this rarely happens, as they are collected from all parts, some far, some near; but the majority too remote to leave the mill for that purpose. After this he is incessantly engaged—not a single minute of rest or relaxation being allowed him.

At twelve o'clock the engine stops, and an hour is given for dinner. The hands leave the mill, and seek their homes, where this meal is usually taken. It consists of potatoes boiled, very often eaten alone; sometimes with a little bacon, and sometimes with a portion of animal food. This latter is, however, only found at the tables of the more provident and reputable workmen. If, as it often happens, the majority of the labourers reside at some distance, a great portion of the allotted time is necessarily taken up by the walk, or rather run, backwards and forwards.

No time is allowed for the observances of ceremony. The meal has been imperfectly cooked, by some one left for that purpose, not unusually a mere child, or superannuated man or woman. The entire family surround the table, if they possess one, each striving which can most rapidly devour the miserable fare before them, which is sufficient, by its quantity, to satisfy the cravings of hunger, but possesses little nutritive quality. . . . As soon as this is effected, the family is again scattered. No rest has been taken; and even the exercise, such as it is, is useless, from its excess, and even harmful, being taken at a time when repose is necessary for the digestive operations.

Again they are closely immured from one o'clock till eight or nine, with the exception of twenty minutes, this being allowed for tea, or baggin-time, as it is called. This imperfect meal is almost universally taken in the mill: it consists of tea and wheaten bread, with very few exceptions. During the whole of this long period they are actively and unremittingly engaged in a crowded room and an elevated temperature, so that, when finally dismissed for the day, they are exhausted equally in body and mind.

It must be remembered that father, mother, son and daughter, are alike engaged; no one capable of working is spared to make home (to which, after a day of such toil and privation, they are hastening) comfortable and desirable. No clean and tidy wife appears to welcome her husband—no smiling and affectionate mother to receive her children—no home, cheerful and inviting, to make it regarded. On the contrary, all assemble there equally jaded; it is miserably furnished—dirty and squalid in its appearance. Another meal, sometimes of a better quality, is now taken, and they either seek that repose which is so much needed, or leave home in pursuit of pleasure or amusements, which still further tend to increase the evils under which they unavoidably labour.

Employment of Children

The subject of child labour roused deep emotion in the 1830s and this emotion has continued to colour our view of the situation to the present. It is important to remember that children had worked long hours under harsh supervision long before the advent of factories and that exploitation of child labour continued in farms and workshops long after it had been brought under control in factories and mines. The employment of children was advantageous to the employer because they were cheap, quick to learn and easy to discipline; for the same reasons women were preferred to men. From the point of view of the labouring classes the employment of children drove down wages but from the point of view of each individual family the employment of each child meant a valuable addition to the total family income. The social implications of child labour defy simple generalisation, although it is certain that the quality of family life suffered severely.

Division of Labour

DOCUMENT 98

Dean Tucker, Instructions to Travellers (1758)

In many Provinces of the Kingdom, particularly Staffordshire, Lancashire, and certain districts of Yorkshire, with the Towns of Manchester, Norwich, and some others, the Labour . . . is very properly proportioned . . . so that no Time shall be wasted in passing the goods to be manufactured from Hand to Hand, and that no unnecessary Strength should be employed. For an instance of both Kinds, take one among a Thousand at Birmingham, viz. When a Man stamps a metal Button by means of an Engine, a Child stands by him to place the Button in readiness to receive the Stamp, and to remove it when received, and then to place another. By these Means the Operator can stamp at least double the Number, which he could otherwise have done, had he been obliged to have stopped each Time to have shifted the Buttons: And as his Gettings may be from 14d to 18d and the Child's from a Penny to 2d per Day for doing the same Quantity of Work, which must have required double the Sum, had the Man alone been employed; this single Circumstance saves alone 80, or even 100 per cent at the same Time that it trains up Children to an Habit of Industry, almost as soon as they can speak. And hence it is that the Bijoux d'Angleterre, or the Birmingham Toys, are rendered so cheap as to astonish all Europe; and that the Roman Catholic countries are supplied with such vast Quantities of Crucifixes, Agnus Dei's, etc. from England. . . . The good Effects of this Proportioning of Labour to different Strengths and Sexes is still more extensive than at first appears. For in Birmingham the Numbers of poor Women on the Pay-Bill, compared to those of Poor Men, are hardly three to two, whereas in Bristol the Numbers are upwards of four to one; and in many parts of London, it is still worse: So great is the Difference, and such is the Expensiveness and heavy Burdens of a Wrong Conduct even in this Respect; not to mention that Prostitution and Debauchery seem to be an unavoidable Consequence in the Female Sex of Poverty and Idleness, when they are young; and when they grow old, what Refuge can they have, if they do not soon rot with their Diseases, but the Parish pay. . . .

Wages and Ages

A. Ure, The Philosophy of Manufactures (1835), p 474

In the cotton factories of Lancashire, the wages of the males during the period when there is the greatest number of employed—from eleven to sixteen—are on the average 4s. 10¾d. a-week; but in the next period of five years, from sixteen to twenty-one, the average rises to 10s. 2½d. a-week; and of course the manufacturer will have as few at that price as he can. . . . In the next period of five years, from twenty-one to twenty-six, the average weekly wages are 17s. 2½d. Here is a still stronger motive to discontinue employing males as far as it can practically be done. In the subsequent two periods the average rises still higher, to 20s. 4½d., and to 22s. 8½d. At such wages, only those men will be employed who are necessary to do work requiring great bodily strength, or great skill, in some art, craft, or mystery . . . or persons employed in offices of trust and confidence.

A Model Employer

DOCUMENT 100

Evidence of a visitor in 1796—Gentleman's Magazine, LXXIV, pp 493-4
Quoted in Mantoux, The Industrial Revolution in the 18th Century, p 467

Four hundred children are entirely fed, clothed and instructed at the expense of this venerable philanthropist. The rest live with their parents in neat comfortable habitations, receiving wages for their labour. The health and happiness depicted on the countenance of these children show that the proprietor of the Lanark mills has remembered mercy in the midst of gain. The regulations here to preserve health of body and mind present a striking contrast to those of most large manufactories in this kingdom, the very hotbeds of contagion and disease. It is a truth that ought to be engraved in letters of gold, to the eternal honour of the founder of New Lanark* that out of nearly three thousand children who have been at work in these mills throughout a period of twelve years, only fourteen have died, and not one has suffered criminal punishment.

* Robert Owen

Effects of Employment

DOCUMENT 101

Mrs Anna Jameson, Memoirs and Essays Illustrative of Art, Literature and Social Morals (1846)

The children—those who survive—grow up to girlhood; as soon as possible they are emancipated, or rather, emancipate themselves, from the domestic control—such as it is—and work for their own maintenance. Those who have the choice, prefer the life of a factory girl to that of a household servant —and they are not far wrong. They have comparative liberty, and work only at stated hours, but they thus acquire with habits of independence, habits of recklessness as regards others; impatience of all quiet, orderly obligations; selfishness, and every kind of unwomanly fault. The Commissioners thus sum up their view of the case:—'It appears that the education of the girls is even more neglected than that of the boys, that the vast majority of females are utterly ignorant; that it is impossible to overrate the evils which result from this deplorable ignorance.'

The unmarried girl, free, reckless, irresponsible, becomes in time the wife and the mother. What is the training that has fitted her for the working man's wife? By the labour of her hands she adds, perhaps, a third to his weekly wages, while, by her carelessness and ignorance of all household duties, she wastes one-half of their united means; or, by her insubordination and unwomanly habits, converts the home into a den of dirt, disquiet, misery. Even when well disposed, the disorderly habits of her childhood and youth leave her no chance but in a strength of character, and a combination of favourable influences, which are at least not common. 'The girls, removed from their home, or from the school to be employed in labour, are prevented from learning needlework, and from acquiring those habits of cleanliness, neatness and order, without which they cannot, when they grow up to womanhood, and have the charge of families of their own, economise their husband's earnings, or give their homes any degree of comfort; and this general want of the qualifications of a housewife in the women of this class, is stated by clergymen, teachers, medical men, employers and other witnesses, to be one great and universally prevailing cause of distress and crime among the working classes!'

Yes; here is the cause—but where is the remedy? If to exist, to procure a pittance of food and decent clothing, a young woman must toil incessantly at some handicraft from five years old and upwards, where and how is she to learn needlework, cookery, economy, cleanliness, and all 'the arts of home?' These things are not taught in Sunday-schools, nor in Dame-schools; and if they were, she has not time to learn them, nor opportunity to apply them, being learned;—she must toil in womanhood as in childhood and girlhood—always toil—toil—unremitting, heart-sickening, soul-and-body-wearing toil! What is the use of instituting a system of education if you continue a state of things in which that education is useless?—which renders it impossible for the woman to practise what the child has learned?—in which incessant labour is the sole condition of existence? The women of these classes have no home—can we wonder they have no morals?

DOCUMENT 102

The Leeds Mercury, Saturday, 16th October 1830

SLAVERY IN YORKSHIRE

To the editors of the Leeds Mercury

'It is the pride of Britain that a Slave cannot exist on her soil; and if I read the genius of her constitution aright, I find that Slavery is most abhorrent to it—that the air which Britons breathe is free—the ground on which they tread is sacred to liberty.'

>   Rev. R. W. Hamilton's Speech at the Meeting held in the Cloth-Hall Yard, Sept. 22nd, 1830.

Gentlemen, No heart responded with truer accents to the sounds of liberty which were heard in the Leeds Cloth-Hall yard, on the 22nd instant, than did mine, and from none could more sincere and earnest prayers arise to the throne of Heaven, that hereafter Slavery might only be known to Britain in the pages of her history. One shade alone obscured my pleasure, arising not from any difference in principle, but from the want of application of the general principle *to the whole Empire*. The proud and able champions of *Negro* liberty and *Colonial* rights should, if I mistake not, have gone farther than they did; or perhaps, to speak more correctly, before they had travelled so far as the West Indies, should, at least for a few moments, have sojourned in our immediate neighbourhood, and have directed the attention of the meeting to scenes of misery, acts of oppression and victims of Slavery, even on the threshold of our homes!

Let the truth speak out, appalling as the statements may appear. The fact is true. Thousands of our fellow-creatures and fellow-subjects, both male and female, the inhabitants of a *Yorkshire-town*, (Yorkshire now represented in Parliament by the giant of anti-slavery principles,*) are at this very moment existing in a state of slavery *more horrid* than are the victims of that hellish system—'Colonial Slavery'. These innocent creatures drawl out unpitied their short but miserable existance in a place famed for its profession of religious zeal, whose inhabitants are ever foremost in *professing* 'Temperance' and 'Reformation', and are striving to outrun their neighbours in Missionary exertions, and would fain send the Bible to the farthest corner of the Globe —aye in the very place where the anti-slavery fever rages most furiously, her *apparent charity* is not more admired on earth, than her *real* cruelty is abhorred in heaven. The very streets which receive the droppings of an 'Anti-Slavery Society' are every morning wet with the tears of innocent victims of the accursed shrine of avarice, who are compelled (not by the

*Brougham,

cart-whip of the negro slave-driver) but by the dread of the equally appalling thong or strap of the overlooker, to hasten half-dressed, *but not half-fed*, to those magazines of British Infantile Slavery—*the Worsted Mills in the town and neighbourhood of Bradford*! ! !

．　　．　　．　　．　　．

Thousands of little children, both male and female, *but principally female*, from SEVEN to fourteen years, are daily *compelled to labour* from six o'clock in the morning to seven in the evening with only—Britons, blush whilst you read it!—*with only thirty minutes allowed for eating and recreation*.

The Blacks may be fairly compared to beasts of burden *kept for their master's use*. The whites to those *which others keep and let for hire*! If I have succeeded in calling the attention of your readers to the horrid and abominable system on which the worsted mills in and near Bradford are conducted, I have done some good. Why should not children working in them be protected by legislative enactments, as well as those who work in cotton mills. Christians should feel and act for those whom Christ so eminently loved and declared that 'of such is the kingdom of heaven'.

Your insertion of the above in the Leeds Mercury, at your earliest convenience, will oblige, Gentlemen,

Your most obedient servant,

Richard Oastler.

Frixby Hall, near Huddersfield, Sept. 29th 1830

The Case for Legislation

DOCUMENT 103

Leeds Intelligencer, 22nd September 1831
Quoted in B. L. Hutchins and A. Harrison, A History of Factory Legislation

RESOLUTIONS PASSED AT A PUBLIC MEETING AT LEEDS

1. That the practice of working young children in mills and factories from twelve to sixteen hours a day, and in some instances thirty-five hours, with but very short intermission for meals, is greatly to be deplored, inasmuch as such a system has an exceedingly pernicious effect on their constitutional vigour, health and morals.

2. That ten hours per day is as long a period for the juvenile population to labour as is consistent with the preservation of health, the allowance of necessary relaxation and rest, and the well-being of society at large, and that it is a stain on the character of Britain that her sons and daughters, in their infant days, should now be worked longer than the adult mechanic, agricultural labourer or negro slave.

4. That a restrictive Act would tend materially to equalise and extend labour, by calling into employment many male adults, who are a burden on the public, who, though willing and ready to work, are obliged, under the existing calamitous system, to spend their time in idleness, whilst female children are compelled to labour from twelve to sixteen hours a day.

A Boy in the Mines

DOCUMENT 104

P.P. Childrens' Employment Commission 1842
Evidence of Nichol Hudderson (Monkwearmouth Colliery)

Sixteen. Is bound as a putter, but unable to put yet. A year ago the horse ran away; knocked him off; trailed with the waggons. Off 10 months. Is lame now, and will always be lame. His leg was set wrong at first. One leg is shorter than the other. The pit makes him sick. Has been very bad in his health ever since he went down the pit. Was very healthy before. Has been here nearly 6 years. This is the sixth year. The heat makes him sick. The sulphur rising up the shaft as he goes down makes his head work. Feels worst when he first goes down in the morning; at 3 o'clock in the morning; and when he comes up at 6 o'clock he feels sick. It is nearly 7 o'clock before he gets home sometimes. It depends on how far he is in bye (how far from the bottom of the shaft). Very seldom when he gets home can he eat very much; this is from the heat and long hours of the pit. Gets to bed at different times. Generally lying down by the fireside first, and sleeping there first. Mother calls him about 3 o'clock; when he feels very sleepy, and often so sick that he cannot eat when he gets up, at least he cannot eat very much. Sometimes he can eat his baits down the pit, sometimes not. Sometimes so sick as to bring up his victuals again from his stomach. Did this twice last week. Most of the boys do this at times, once in a week at the least perhaps. About half a year since, a lad, John Huggins, was very sick down the pit, and wanted to come up, but the keeper would not let him ride (come up), and he died of a fever one week after. (The father of this lad and his brother fully corroborate this statement; and the father says the doctor told him if he (the boy) had not been kept in the pit he might have been, perhaps, saved. This boy had never had anything the matter with him before he went down the pit). Knows some boys who have been sick in this way. Has known three boys killed about 4 years ago. The rope broke when the corf was going down, and they fell to the bottom: the rope falling on top of them.

A Defence of Mine-work

P.P. Childrens' Employment Commission 1842
Evidence of Henry Morton, of Biddick, near Lambton

Agent for the Countess of Durham's collieries. Thinks that the usual employment of the children in coal mines is perfectly consistent with their health. Making very good wages, they are enabled to have good and sufficient maintenance. Working at the night shift does not make much difference, the air and ventilation being the same at one period as at another; does not think the changing the night into day in any way injures them. Within an experience of about 14 years in the Countess of Durham's mines, has not observed any instances of prejudicial effects from the hours, or mode or place of working. . . . Has never heard of any boys straining or rupturing themselves in these pits. Does not think any alteration in the hours of labour necessary for children. Would not object to a law restricting children from going down before 10 years old, but would rather leave it to the discretion of the viewer to accept or refuse them; any such law would press heavily on parents who had large families. Any medical and educational certificates would be totally unnecessary. Does not think the means of education now open to the boys are at all sufficient, but the reverse, quite insufficient. Parents are anxious to send children to school, but they have no good schools; and boys might obtain instruction, after going to work, if there were proper arrangements for diffusing it. Does not think that the work in the pit incapacitates them to receive instruction after the day's labour, especially with regard to putters, who usually work only 8 hours, or at least they may usually be done within that time. . . .

There is no prospect of any mode of carrying on collieries so as to dispense with the labours of very young children; any restricting law that should produce a scarcity of children would prevent many pits from being carried on beneficially; old men, to supplant trappers, and what are called swing doors, are inapplicable. Pitmen become perhaps thin, but are extremely active and muscular, and are in general quite as healthy as other labourers; of course they are subject to accidents. Does not think pit-people are necessarily lower in stature than others, and their work does not produce that effect. They consider themselves vastly superior, in the scale of society, to agricultural labourers. Drunkenness is a prevalent vice, and dog-fighting is a favourable amusement.

DOCUMENT 106

Children's Employment Commission Mines 1842 (XV), p 255

CONCLUSIONS

From the whole of the evidence which has been collected, and of which we have thus endeavoured to give a digest, we find—

In regard to Coal Mines—

1. That instances occur in which children are taken into these mines to work as early as four years of age, sometimes at five, and between five and six, not unfrequently between six and seven, and often from seven to eight, while from eight to nine is the ordinary age at which employment in these mines commences.

2. That a very large proportion of the persons employed in carrying on the work of these mines is under thirteen years of age; and a still larger proportion between thirteen and eighteen.

3. That in several districts female children begin work in these mines at the same early ages as the males.

7. That the nature of the employment which is assigned to the youngest children, generally that of 'trapping', requires that they should be in the pit as soon as the work of the day commences, and, according to the present system, that they should not leave the pit before the work of the day is at an end.

8. That although this employment scarcely deserves the name of labour, yet, as the children engaged in it are commonly excluded from light and are always without companions, it would, were it not for the passing and re-passing of the coal carriages, amount to solitary confinement of the worst order.

9. That in those districts in which the seams of coal are so thick that horses go direct to the workings, or in which the side passages from the workings to the horseways are not of any great length, the lights in the mainways render the situation of these children comparatively less cheerless, dull and stupefying; but that in some districts they remain in solitude and darkness during the whole time they are in the pit, and, according to their own account, many of them never see the light of day for weeks together during the greater part of the winter season, excepting on those days in the week when work is not going on, and on the Sundays.

10. That at different ages, from six years old and upwards, the hard work of pushing and dragging the carriages of coal from the workings to the main ways or to the foot of the shaft begins; a labour which all classes of witnesses concur in stating requires the unremitting exertion of all the physical power which the young workers possess.

11. That, in the districts in which females are taken down into the coal

mines, both sexes are employed together in precisely the same kind of labour, and work for the same number of hours; that the girls and boys, and the young men and young women, and even married women and women with child, commonly work almost naked, and the men, in many mines, quite naked; and that all classes of witnesses bear testimony to the demoralising influence of the employment of females underground.

13. That when the workpeople are in full employment, the regular hours of work for children and young persons are rarely less than eleven; more often they are twelve; in some districts they are thirteen; and in one district they are generally fourteen and upwards.

14. That in the great majority of these mines night-work is a part of the ordinary system of labour, more or less regularly carried on according to the demand for coals, and one which the whole body of evidence shows to act most injuriously both on the physical and moral condition of the workpeople, and more especially on that of the children and young persons.

Wages

Case for Low Wages

DOCUMENT 107

J. Smith, Memoirs of Wool (1747), II, p 308

It is a fact well known ... that scarcity, to a certain degree, promotes industry, and that the manufacturer who can subsist on three days work will be idle and drunken the remainder of the week. . . . The poor in the manufacturing counties will never work any more time in general than is necessary just to live and support their weekly debauches. . . . We can fairly aver that a reduction of wages in the woollen manufacture would be a national blessing and advantage, and no real injury to the poor. By this means we might keep our trade, uphold our rents, and reform the people into the bargain.

High Wages in England

DOCUMENT 108

N. Senior, Ground and Objects of the Budget
Quoted in Coats, 'The Classical Economists and the Labourer' in 'Land,
Labour and Population in the Industrial Revolution,' ed. Jones & Mingay,
pp 114–15

To complain of our high wages is to complain that our labour is productive—to complain that our workpeople are diligent and skilful. To act on such complaints is as wise as to enact that all men should labour with only one hand, or stand idle four days in every week. . . . The well-directed labour of an Englishman is worth twice as much as that of any inhabitant of Europe; it is worth four or five times as much as the labour of the less advantaged European districts; and it is worth twelve or fifteen times as much as the labour of the most civilised Asiatic nations.

. . . . . .

When wages are high, they work fewer hours and inhabit better houses; and, if there still remain a superfluity the women and girls waste it in dress, and the men in drink or luxurious living. When wages fall, they endeavour to increase their earnings by more assiduous labour, and to economise, first in house-rent, then in dress, then in fuel, and ultimately in food. When their earnings become insufficient for a maintenance, they throw themselves on the parish. The virtue of which they possess the least is providence.

Self-Help and Saving

DOCUMENT 109

Mr William Felkin of Nottingham to the British Association meeting at Liverpool
Quoted in Porter, Progress of the Nation, p 455

If any one intends to improve his condition, he must earn all he can, spend as little as he can, and make what he does spend bring him and his family all the real enjoyments he can. The first saving which a working man effects out of his earnings, is the first step, and because it is the first step, the most important step towards true independence. Now independence is as practicable in the case of an industrious and economic, though originally poor workman, as in that of the tradesman or merchant, and is as great and estimable a blessing. The same process must be attended to, i.e., the entire expenditure being kept below the clear income, all contingent claims being carefully considered and provided for, and the surplus held sacred to be employed for those purposes, and those only, which duty and conscience may point out as important or desirable. This requires a course of laborious exertion and strict economy, a little foresight, and possibly some privation. But this is only what is common to the acquisition of all desirable objects. And inasmuch as I know what it is to labour with the hands long hours, and for small wages, as well as any workman to whom I address myself, and to practise self-denial withal, I am emboldened to declare from experience, that the gain of independence, or rather self-dependence, for which I plead, is worth infinitely more than all the cost of its attainment; and moreover, that to attain it, in a greater or less degree, according to circumstances, is within the power of far the greater number

of skilled workmen engaged in our manufactures. Unhappily, the earnings
of the industrious workpeople in some trades have been at times, and often
for a long time, so scanty as to afford scarcely the means of existence. The
hand-loom weavers and common stocking-makers have been very dis-
tressing cases of this kind, but they have been exceptions, and most power-
fully establish the general position for instances have not been of unfrequent
occurrence in both these trades, of workmen, by dint of perseverance and
economy, emerging from the mass of misery around them, and placing
themselves in easy and happy circumstances.' |

Credit

DOCUMENT 110

*Report of Select Committee on Manufactures and Trade (1883), Q.10566–71
Quoted in Davis, A History of Shops and Shopping*

Q. What are the habits of the people dealing at the retail shops? Do they
deal mostly for ready money or upon credit?

A. I should think that one half of the commodities purchased by the
labouring people of Stockport for domestic purposes of every kind are
purchased on credit.

Q. What length of credit?

A. With the retail shopmen of the town who sell food, it is generally
from week to week.

Q. Is there any difference in price between cash and tick?

A. Yes. From 2s. to 4s. in the pound. But I estimate it in more ways than
by the money paid. When a person begins with a huckster he is generally
more inclined to consume above his income than when he has to pay ready
money. He generally gets bound to the huckster, and when it is so, he
cannot always insist upon having the weight or an article of the proper
quality, and it is always higher in price besides, 2d. or 3d. for a dozen of
flour, and about a penny a pound for sugar, and so on.

Q. Is not irregular work the reason for getting into debt to shopkeepers?

A. I think there are more persons who continue it for want of a little
prudence than what are compelled to it by necessity. Those who are actually
poor are more induced to go to a ready money shop on account of having
more commodities for the little money they have to spend.

Q. Is there a distinction between ready money shops and shops giving
credit?

A. Yes. Some ready money shops refuse all credit to the labouring
population.

Outside the Factories

Workshops and Sweatshops

DOCUMENT 111

W. Thompson, Tour of England and Scotland (1788), pp 18–19
Quoted in Asa Briggs, How They Lived 1700–1815

It is not above seventy years since there was any great variety of metal goods fabricated here. Coarse locks and hinges, with common metal buttons and buckles, formed before that period, the whole amount of the Birmingham manufactures. But now, these coarse articles are manufactured in Wolverhampton, Walsall, Dudley, and other small towns near Birmingham. The fine and fashionable goods are manufactured in the town of Birmingham itself. In the country around about are nailers and woodscrew-makers, who work in their own cottages, and whose prices are so low, that they get but very little money by all their labour. The women and children, as well as the men are employed in the manufacture of these articles. Sometimes the whole family will be occupied in one branch of business, which suits well enough, as the father of the family makes large nails, and the wife and children smaller ones according to their strength. This division of labour in the same family, if studied and practised in different kinds of British manufactures, might in this country, as in India, expedite business, and also improve the articles produced by it.

The industry of the people in those parts is wonderful. They live here like the people of Spain and other hot countries, rising at three or four o'clock in the morning, going to rest for a few hours at noon, and afterwards working till nine or ten o'clock at night.

It is exceedingly remarkable, and highly worthy of observation, that industry in manufactures in the district adjacent to Birmingham, is wholly confined to the barren parts of the country. This great town stands on the south-east extremity of a very barren region . . . [On the] west, where the ground is fertile and well cultivated, there is scarcely a manufacturer to be found of any kin.'

Wodgate

DOCUMENT 112

Benjamin Disraeli, Sybil (1845)

The business of Wodgate is carried on by master workmen in their own houses, each of whom possesses an unlimited number of what they call apprentices, by whom their affairs are principally conducted, and whom they treat as the Mamlouks treated the Egyptians. These master workmen indeed form a powerful aristocracy, nor is it possible to conceive one apparently more oppressive. Their youths are worked for sixteen and even twenty hours a-day, they are often sold by one master to another; they are fed on carrion and they sleep in lofts or cellars: yet whether it be that they are hardened by brutality, and really unconscious of their degradation and unusual sufferings, or whether they are supported by the belief that their day to be masters and oppressors will surely arrive, the aristocracy of Wodgate is by no means so unpopular as the aristocracy of most other places.

In the first place it is a real aristocracy; it is privileged, but it does something for its privileges. It is distinguished from the main body not merely by name. It is the most knowing class at Wodgate; it possesses indeed in its way complete knowledge; and it imparts in its manner a certain quantity of it to those whom it guides. Thus it is an aristocracy that leads and therefore a fact. Moreover the social system of Wodgate is not an unvarying course of infinite toil. Their plan is to work hard, but not always. They seldom exceed four days of labour in the week. On Sunday the masters begin to drink; for the apprentices there is dog-fighting without any stint. On Monday and Tuesday the whole population of Wodgate is drunk; of all stations, ages and sexes; even babes, who should be at the breast; for they are drammed with Godfrey's cordial. Here is relaxation, excitement; if less vice otherwise than might at first be anticipated, we must remember that excesses are checked by poverty of blood and constant exhaustion. Scanty food and hard labour are in their way, if not exactly moralists, tolerably good police.

There are no others at Wodgate to preach or to control. It is not that the people are immoral, for immorality implies some forethought; or ig-norant, for ignorance is relative; but they are animals; unconscious; their minds a blank; and their worst actions only the impulse of a gross or savage instinct. There are many in this town who are ignorant of their very names; very few who can spell them. It is rare that you meet with a young person who knows his own age; rarer to find the boy who has seen a book, or the girl who has seen a flower. Ask them the name of their sovereign, and they will give you an unmeaning stare; ask them the name of their religion, and they will laugh: who rules them on earth, or who can save them in Heaven, are alike mysteries to them.

Such was the population with whom Morley was about to mingle.

Wodgate had the appearance of a vast squalid suburb. As you advanced leaving behind you long lines of little dingy tenements, with infants lying about the road, you expected every moment to emerge into some streets and encounter buildings bearing some correspondence in their size and comfort to the considerable population swarming and busied around you. Nothing of the kind. There were no public buildings of any sort; no churches, chapels, town-halls, institute, theatre; and the principal streets in the heart of the town in which were situate the coarse and grimy shops, though formed by houses of a greater elevation than the preceding, were equally narrow and if possible more dirty. At every fourth or fifth house, alleys seldom above a yard wide and streaming with filth, opened out of the street. These were crowded with dwellings of various size, while from the principal court often branched out a number of smaller alleys or rather narrow passages, than which nothing can be conceived more close and squalid and obscure. Here during the days of business, the sound of the hammer and the file never ceased, amid gutters of abomination and piles of foulness and stagnant pools of filth; reservoirs of leprosy and plague, whose exhalations were sufficient to taint the atmosphere of the whole kingdom and fill the country with fever and pestilence.

Sweat Shop

DOCUMENT 113

Charles Kingsley, Alton Locke (1850)

I stumbled after Mr Jones up a dark, narrow iron staircase till we emerged through a trap-door into a garret at the top of the house. I recoiled with disgust at the scene before me; and here I was to work—perhaps through life! A low lean-to room, stifling me with the combined odours of human breath and perspiration, stale beer, the sweet sickly smell of gin, and the sour and hardly less disgusting one of new cloth. On the floor, thick with dust and dirt, scraps of stuff and ends of thread, sat some dozen haggard, untidy, shoeless men, with a mingled look of care and recklessness that made me shudder. The windows were tight closed to keep out the cold winter air; and the condensed breath ran in streams down the panes, chequering the dreary outlook of chimney-tops and smoke.

Casual Labour

The Irish

DOCUMENT 114

Report of the State of the Irish Poor in Great Britain (1836), pp v, vii–ix
Quoted in E. P. Thompson, The Making of the English Working Class,
pp 473–6

THE WORK THEY DID:

. . . the most irksome and disagreeable kinds of coarse labour, such for instance as attending on masons, bricklayers and plasterers, excavating earth for harbours, docks, canals and roads, carrying heavy goods, loading and unloading vessels.

EVIDENCE OF A BIRMINGHAM EMPLOYER:

'The Irish labourers will work any time. . . . I consider them very valuable labourers, and we could not do without them. By treating them kindly, they will do anything for you. . . . An English man could not do the work they do. When you push them they have a willingness to oblige which the English have not; they would die under anything before they would be beat; they would go at hard work till they drop before a man should excel them. . . .

EVIDENCE OF A BUILDING EMPLOYER:

They scarcely ever make good mechanics; they don't look deep into subjects; their knowledge is quick but superficial; they don't make good millwrights or engineers, or anything which requires thought.

CONCLUSION OF THE REPORT:

The Irish emigration into Britain is an example of a less civilised population spreading themselves, as a kind of substratum, beneath a more civilised community; and without excelling in any branch of industry, obtaining possession of all the lowest departments of manual labour.

The Navvies

DOCUMENT 115

J. R. Francis, A History of the English Railway (1851)

Rude, rugged and uncultivated, possessed of great animal strength, collected in large numbers, living and working entirely together, they are a class and a community by themselves. Before the time of that great Duke who called inland navigation into existence, this class was unknown; and in the works which bear witness to his forethought, the 'navigator' gained his title. The canal manias which ensued created a demand and increased the body: the great architectural works of the kingdom continued it; and when the rail first began to spread its iron road through England, the labour attracted no attention from politician or philosopher, from statistician or statesman; he had joined no important body, he had not made himself an object of dread; Rough, alike in morals and in manners, collected from the wild hills of Yorkshire and Lancashire, coming in troops from the fens of Lincolnshire, and afterwards pouring in masses from every country in the empire; displaying an unbending vigour and an independent bearing; mostly dwelling apart from the villagers near whom they worked; with all the propensities of an untaught, undisciplined nature; unable to read and unwilling to be taught; impetuous, impulsive and brute-like, regarded as the pariahs of private life, herding together like beasts of the field, owning no moral law and feeling no social tie, they increased with an increased demand, and from thousands grew to hundreds of thousands. They lived but for the present; they cared not for the past, they were indifferent to the future.

The inquiry instituted by Parliament elicited information which surprised some and revolted all. . . . They earned high wages, and they spent them. They worked hard and they lived well. The waste of power which their daily labour necessitated, was supplied by an absorption of stimulant and nourishment perfectly astounding. . . . They were in a state of utter barbarism. They made their houses where they got their work. Some slept in huts constructed of damp turf, cut from the wet grass, too low to stand upright in; while small sticks, covered with straw, served as rafters. . . . It mattered not to them that the rain beat through the roof, and that the wind swept through the holes. If they caught a fever, they died; if they took an infectious complaint, they wandered in the open air, spreading the disease wherever they went. . . . Many of them lived in a state of intoxication until their money was spent, and they were again obliged to have recourse to labour. . . .

The Street Folk

DOCUMENT 116

H. Mayhew, London Labour and the London Poor (1851) (ed. Quennell, p 29)

Of the thousand millions of human beings that are said to constitute the population of the entire globe, there are—socially, morally, and perhaps even physically considered—but two distinct and broadly marked races viz., the wanderers and the settlers—the vagabond and the citizen—the nomadic and the civilised tribes.

The nomadic races of England are of many distinct kinds—from the habitual vagrant—half-beggar, half-thief—sleeping in barns, tents, and casual wards—to the mechanic on tramp, obtaining his bed and supper from the trade societies in the different towns, on his way to seek work. Between these two extremes there are several mediate varieties—consisting of pedlars, showmen, harvestmen, and all that large class who live by either selling, showing, or doing something through the country. These are, so to speak, the rural nomads—not confining their wanderings to any one particular locality, but ranging often from one end of the land to the other. Besides these, there are the urban and suburban wanderers, or those who follow some itinerant occupation in and around about the large towns. Such are, in the metropolis more particularly, the pick-pockets—the beggars—the prostitutes—the street-sellers—the street-performers—the cabmen—the coachmen—the watermen—the sailors and such like.

Those who obtain their living in the streets of the metropolis are a very large and varied class; indeed, the means resorted to in order 'to pick up a crust', as the people call it, in the public thoroughfares (and such in many instances it literally is) are so multifarious that the mind is long baffled in its attempts to reduce them to scientific order or classification.

It would appear, however, that the street-people may be all arranged under six distinct genera or kinds.

These are severally:

I. Street-sellers   IV. Street-performers, Artists & Showmen
II. Street-buyers   V. Street-Artisans or Working Pedlars
III. Street-finders   VI. Street-Labourers

From Job to Job

DOCUMENT 117

B. Wilson, The Struggles of an Old Chartist and A Quarryman (1887), p 13
Quoted in E. P. Thompson, The Making of the English Working Class, p 275

Tom Brown's Schooldays would have had no charm for me, as I had never been to a day school in my life; when very young I had to begin working, and was pulled out of bed between 4 and 5 o'clock . . . in summer time to go with a donkey 1½ miles away, and then take part in milking a number of cows; and in the evening had again to go with milk and it would be 8 o'clock before I had done. I went to a card shop afterwards and there had to set 1,500 card teeth for a ½d. From 1842 to 1848 I should not average 9/- per week wages; outdoor and labour was bad to get then and wages were very low. I have been a woollen weaver, a comber, a navvy on the railway, and a barer in the delph* that I claim to know some little of the state of the working classes.

* a quarryman.

The Proportion of Casuals

DOCUMENT 118

Mayhew, London Labour and the London Poor, II, pp 364–5

. . . estimating the working classes as being between four and five million in number, I think we may safely assert—considering how many depend for their employment on particular times, seasons, fashions, and accidents, and the vast quantity of over-work and scamp-work in nearly all the cheap trades . . . the number of women and children who are being continually drafted into the different handicrafts with the view of reducing the earnings of the men, the displacement of human labour in some cases by machinery . . . all these things being considered I say I believe that we may safely conclude that . . . there is barely sufficient work for the regular employment of half of our labourers, so that only 1,500,000 are fully and constantly employed, while 1,500,000 more are employed only half their time, and the remaining 1,500,000 wholly unemployed, obtaining a day's work occasionally by the displacement of some of the others.

The Organisation of Labour

Preface

The mechanisation of manufacture and the introduction of new, intensive techniques of cultivation in agriculture, increased the ratio of capital to labour in the processes of production. Fewer men could look forward to becoming their own masters and an increasing number of employers could forget the time when they were workmen. Remnants of paternalism lingered in factory feasts and 'wakes' but the relationship between men and employers changed and hardened. Capital created a social and mental gulf which found expression in a new vocabulary of socialism, which gave form and expression to the new class-consciousness which social and economic pressures had forged. As old notions of social obligation and the 'just price', exemplified in the attitudes of generations of food-rioters, faded away, they were replaced by the realisation that agglomerations of capital, which had the power to determine the conditions and even the possibility of employment, had to be faced by combinations of labour, organised to wring concessions from an employing class whose interests were conveived of as directly opposed to those of their employees.

The progress of unionism in the first half of the century was not spectacular. The difficulties confronting would-be organisers were immense—illiteracy, lack of funds, hostile courts, and a labour market flooded with young adults, small children and growing numbers of Celtic immigrants. The distractions of political reform and the attractions of respectable status, to be achieved by diligent self-improvement, lured away many potential leaders of effective labour organisations. Frustration found outlets in machine-smashing, 'bargaining by riot' and bitter, but fruitless strikes. Only among skilled, literate workers, who were able to accumulate a strike fund and threaten a damaging withdrawal of labour, did lasting union organisation take root.

Food Riots

DOCUMENT 119

From the Annual Register (1766), Chronicle, pp 137–40

There having been many riots, and much mischief done, in different parts of England, in consequence of the rising of the poor; who have been driven to desperation and madness, by the exorbitant prices of all manner of provisions; we shall, without descending to minute particulars, or a strict regard as to the order of time, in which they happened, give a short abstract of those disturbances.

At Bath, the people did a great deal of mischief in the markets before they dispersed.

They were very outrageous at Berwick upon Tweed, on account of the vast quantities of corn that had been bought up for exportation.

At Malmesbury they seized all the corn; sold it at 5s. a bushel, and gave the money to the right owners.

At Hampton, in Gloucestershire, they were opposed, some lives were lost and houses pulled down, and the military called in to quell them.

. . . . .

At Leicester, and the neighbourhood, they seized three waggon-loads of cheese, and divided them among them.

At Lechdale, they seized a waggon-load of cheese, designed for London, and carried it all off; and not content with that, broke open the warehouses of the owners, and robbed them of five or six tons more.

. . . . .

At Gloucester, the most considerable farmers from the hills voluntarily agreed to supply the market with wheat at 5s. a bushel, and have already sold considerable quantities at that price.

At Salisbury, the risings were very serious, and much damage was expected, but by the prudent management of the magistrates, and the humanity of the farmers, who lowered the price of their wheat on the first disturbance, the danger was happily averted. Some of the ringleaders, however, were apprehended and committed to prison.

At Beckington, near Bath, a miller and his son got fire-arms to oppose the mob, and actually fired and killed a man and a boy, and desperately wounded others, which so exasperated the rest, that they set fire to the mills, and burnt them to the ground.

. . . . .

At Norwich a general insurrection began, when the proclamation was read in the market-place, where provisions of all sorts were scattered about by the rioters in heaps; the new mill, a spacious building, which supplies the city with water, was attacked and pulled down; the flour, to the number of 150 sacks, thrown, sack after sack, into the river; and the proprietor's books of account, furniture, plate, and money, carried off or destroyed; the bakers' shops plundered and shattered; a large malt-house set fire to, and burnt; houses and warehouses pulled down; and the whole city thrown into the greatest consternation. During this scene of confusion, the magistrates issued out summonses to the housekeepers in their respective districts, to assemble with staves to oppose the rioters; the conflict was long and bloody, but, in the end, the rioters were overpowered, thirty of the ringleaders secured and committed to prison, who, it is said, will soon be tried by a special commission.

.　　　.　　　.　　　.　　　.

At Great-Colton in Warwickshire they rose, traversed the country, and did considerable damage, till being met by the military, they were encountered and dispersed, eight of them having been shot dead before they reached Kidderminster.

The Grievances of Labour

DOCUMENT 120

From Revolutions without Bloodshed, or Reformation Preferable to Revolt (1794)
Quoted in Cole and Filson, British Working Class Movements

It having been industriously asserted that the happiness and prosperity of the people would not be at all increased by a Reform of the Representation, it has been thought proper to publish the following enumeration of those changes which in all probability might be thereby produced.
I
The CLAIMS OF THE PEOPLE might be more duly attended to, and their RIGHTS restored.
II
Taxes might be proportioned to the abilities of those upon whom they are levied, and not made to fall heavier on the *poor* than on the *rich*.
III
The present system of Excising almost all the *necessaries of life*, as soap, candles, starch, beer, etc., etc., might be abolished.
IV
The POOR LAWS AND LAWS OF SETTLEMENTS might be amended, and a poor man not be liable to be sent to prison for moving out of his own parish to seek employment.

V

The GAME LAWS might be abolished, and the farmer be no longer obliged to permit his rich and insolent neighbour to trample his fields in pursuit of an animal, which, though fed by the produce of his own grounds, the farmer himself dares not kill, but under the penalty of fine and imprisonment.

VI

Workmen might no longer be punished with imprisonment for uniting to obtain an increase of wages, whilst their masters are allowed to conspire against them with impunity.

X

The RICH might be prevented from swelling their excessive incomes by MONOPOLISING the necessities of life, and even the farms by which they are produced.

XI

Some NATIONAL ESTABLISHMENT might yield to the *Children of the Poor* such instruction as might enable them to *earn their living*, and form a just notion of their *rights* and *duties* as members of society.

XII

CONSTANT EMPLOY might be secured to the *industrious*, and due PROVISION be made for the *aged* and *disabled*.

XIII

Families that are comparatively starving might be exempted from contributing towards the enormous sums squandered on *unmerited* SALARIES and PENSIONS.

XIV

The UNFORTUNATE TRADESMAN, ruined, perhaps by some swindler of rank, might not be consigned to the horrors of a dungeon, because oppressed by the heavy hand of misfortune.

XV

A poor and industrious man might no longer be prevented from getting his living by the various inclusive Franchises, Privileges and Charters of different Trades and Corporations, shutting him out from exercising perhaps the only trade he is capable of, and perhaps from the only spot where he might hope for success.

Petition for Laws Against Combinations

DOCUMENT 121

Petition of London Master Millwrights, 1799
Quoted in P. W. Kingsford, Engineers, Inventors and Workers

A dangerous combination has for some time existed among the Journeymen Millwrights, within the metropolis, and the limits of 25 miles round the same, for enforcing a general increase in their wages, preventing the employment of such journeymen as refuse to join their confederacy, and for other illegal purposes. Frequent conspiracies of this sort have been set on foot by the journeymen, and the masters have been so often obliged to submit, and that a demand for a further increase in wages has recently been made, which, not being complied with, the men, within the limits aforesaid, have refused to work; and a compliance with such a demand for an advance of wages hath generally been followed by further claims, with which it is impossible for the masters to comply, without occasioning so considerable advance in the price of mill work as most materially to affect the said business; and that in support of the said combination, the journeymen have established a general fund and raised subscriptions, and so regular and connected is their system that their demands are sometimes made regularly by all the journeymen at the same time, and at other times at some particular shop, and, in the case of non-compliance, the different workshops are wholly deserted by the men, and the journeymen are prohibited from applying for work until the master millwrights are brought to compliance, and the journeymen who have thus thrown themselves out of employ receive support meanwhile from their general fund.

And therefore praying that leave may be given to exhibit a petition for leave to bring in a Bill, for the better preventing the unlawful combinations of workmen employed in the millwright business, and for regulating the wages of such workmen, in such a manner as the House shall deem meet.

Solidarity

DOCUMENT 122

A Letter from the Liverpool Union, dated 14th November 1803
Quoted in J. L. and Barbara Hammond, The Town Labourer

LOVING SHOPMAITES,—I hope you will Excuse our neglect in not wrighting before now to return you our grateful thanks for your timely asistance in our last contest with our tyrant, hopeing you will retain the same regard wich you have shown in your last contribushion towards us at a time when we was so much nesseated at any time should any thing of the kind happen to you you lose no time to inform us of your sittuashion that we may shew ourselfs as much in your intrest and well faire as lyes in our power as we still and allways shall think our indeted to you for the suploys we received from you without wich we must a suffered verrey much as we did not receive the suploys from the other towns as we Expected, but since we have got partley through our distresses we hope you will not omitt wrighting to us as we shall be obliged to you for your asistance in all cases to conduct us as we are but indriffriently sittuated for we have so maney disarters the cause on a count of contribushions but this we dispise for it a man will not contribute to the suport of his fellow shopmates he is better at a distance than preasant.

Amongst disarters Wm. Hall our last president wo has gone to phillipps purposley to instruct his aprentises on acount of wich he is going to ogment them to 30 he is hired for som time at so much pr week to instruct 2 boys at one time and John Welch and Thomas Richards and all the others has reduced there wages 2 pence pr paire wich we you will make as publick through your meetings what villands we have had amongst us—I suppose you have heared of the death of Mr. Taylor our last clark wich has put us much about or we should a rote before.

P.S.—at the request of Mr. Richardson our Seckeretary I was to inform you of the conduct of Charles Duggeon wo with 2 others dubblin Boot men has gone to our tyrant phillipps a longue with the other scabbs So I conclude hopeing this will find you in good health.

I remain your truley,

in defence of the trade,

FYR. CAPPER

THOS. FREASON
Clark

Ineffectiveness of the Combination Laws

DOCUMENT 123

Place MSS 27,834 f 108, 1834
Quoted in Cole and Filson, British Working Class Movements

I have now before me tables of weekly wages of journeymen tradesmen in London, who in their different trades may amount to 100,000 men, all of whom had separate trade clubs for many years, and spite of the Combination Laws, did from time to time raise their wages by means of strikes.

In these trades the ordinary wages in the year 1777 were from eighteen shillings to twenty two shillings a week—From 1777 to 1794 there were few strikes and very little advance in wages. During this the price of food rose somewhat, but the price of most other necessaries fell and wages were nearly stationary—Soon after the commencement of the war against the French Republic prices rose enormously—and in one of these trades, a very numerous trade (Breeches-making)—a strike took place in 1795 when the weekly wages were raised from twenty two shillings to twenty five shillings. In 1802 another strike raised the wages to thirty shillings. In 1810 another strike raised the wages to thirty three shillings, and in 1813 another strike raised the wages to thirty six shillings at which they have remained ever since. The journeymen in the other trades by their strikes raised their wages in a similar portion, though not precisely at the same periods.

DOCUMENT 124

The Declaration of the Framework Knitters, Home Office Papers 42/119
Quoted in Cole and Filson, op. cit.

Whereas the charter granted by our late sovereign Lord Charles the Second
by the Grace of God King of Great Britain France and Ireland, the Framework knitters are empowered to break and destroy all Frames and Engines
that fabricate articles in a fraudulent and deceitful manner and to destroy all
Framework knitters' Goods whatsoever that are so made and whereas a
number of deceitful unprincipled and intriguing persons did attain an Act
to be passed in the Twenty Eighth Year of our present sovereign Lord George
the Third whereby it was enacted that persons entering by force into any
House Shop or Place to break or destroy Frames should be adjudged guilty
of Felony and as we are fully convinced that such Act was obtained in the
most fraudulent interested and electioneering maner [*sic*] and thet the
Honorable [*sic*] the Parliament of Great Britain was deceived as to the motives
and intentions of the persons who obtained such Act we therefore the
Framework knitters do hereby declare the aforesaid Act to be null and void
to all intents and purposes whatsoever as by the passing of this act villainous
and imposing persons are enabled to make fraudulent and deceitful manufactures to the discredit and utter ruin of our Trade. And whereas we declare
that the aforementioned Charter is as much in force as though no such
Act had been passed. . . . And we do hereby declare to all Hosiers Lace
Manufacturers and proprietors or Frames that we will break and destroy
all manner of Frames whatsoever that make the following spurious articles
and all Frames whatsoever that do not pay the regular prices heretofore
agreed to [by] the Masters and Workmen—All print net Frames making
single press and Frames not working by the rack and rent and not paying
the price regulated in 1810, Warp frames working single yarn or two
coarse hole—not working by the rack, not paying the rent and prices
regulated in 1809—whereas all plain silk Frames not making work according
to the gage—Frames not marking the work according to quality, whereas
all Frames of whatsoever description the workmen of whom are not paid
in the current coin of the realm will invariably be destroyed. . . .

Given under my hand this first day of January 1812
God protect the Trade   Ned Lud's Office
                                           Sherwood Forest.

An Ode to the Framers of the Frame Bill by Lord Byron (1812)
Quoted in The Common Muse, V. de Sola Pinto (ed.)

Oh, well done Lord E(ldo)n! and better done R(yde)r!
    Britannia must prosper with councils like yours;
Hawkesbury, Harrowby, help to guide her,
    Whose remedy only must kill ere it cures:
Those villains; the Weavers, are all grown refractory,
    Asking some succour for Charity's sake—
So hang them in clusters round each Manufactory,
    That will at once put an end to mistake.

The rascals, perhaps, may betake them to robbing,
    The dogs to be sure have got nothing to eat—
So if we can hang them for breaking a bobbin,
    'T will save all the Government's money and meat:
Men are more easily made than machinery—
    Stockings fetch better prices than lives—
Gibbets on Sherwood will heighten the scenery,
    Shewing how Commerce, how Liberty thrives!

Justice is now in pursuit of the wretches,
    Grenadiers, Volunteers, Bow-street Police,
Twenty-two Regiments, a score of Jack Ketches,
    Three of the Quorum and two of the Peace;
Some Lords, to be sure, would have summoned the Judges,
    To take their opinion, but that they ne'er shall,
For LIVERPOOL such a concession begrudges,
    So now they're condemned by no Judges at all.

Some folks for certain have thought it was shocking,
    When Famine appeals and when Poverty groans,
That Life should be valued at less than a stocking,
    And breaking of frames lead to breaking of bones.
If it should prove so, I trust, by this token,
    (And who will refuse to partake in the hope?)
That the frames of the fools may be first to be broken,
    Who, when asked for a remedy, sent down a rope.

Lord Byron Speaks Against Oppression
27th February 1812 (Hansard, xxi, 966–72)

. . . nothing but absolute want could have driven a large, and once honest and industrious, body of the people, into the commission of excesses so hazardous. . . . You call these men a mob. . . . Are we aware of our obligations to a mob? It is the mob that labour in your fields and serve in your houses, that man your navy, and recruit your army, that have enabled you to defy all the world, and can also defy you when neglect and calamity have driven them to despair. . . . I have traversed the seat of war in the peninsula, I have been in some of the most oppressed provinces of Turkey, but never under the most despotic of infidel governments did I behold such squalid wretchedness as I have seen since my return in the very heart of a Christian country. And what are your remedies? After months of inaction, and months of action worse than inactivity, at length comes forth the grand specific, the never failing nostrum of all state physicians, from the days of Draco to the present time . . . death . . . Is there not blood enough upon your penal code, that more must be poured forth to ascend to Heaven and testify against you? . . . Are these the remedies for a starving and desperate populace?

The New Labour Force

Robert Owen (1771–1858) started work at the age of ten, and by the time he was nineteen he was a mill manager. His work as a manager of labour led him, after he had made his own fortune out of cotton, to interest himself in schemes for the improvement of the life of the labouring classes. He believed in the fundamental goodness of man and was convinced that social problems could be eradicated by the provision of a suitable environment, and to this end he established model communities at New Lanark in Scotland and Harmony Hall in America. He also played a prominent part in the union movement. As he grew older, however, he alienated many potential sympathisers by his avowed atheism and increasingly socialistic beliefs.

DOCUMENT 127

Robert Owen, Observations on the Effect of the Manufacturing System (1815) Quoted in Cole and Filson, British Working Class Movements

Those who were engaged in the trade, manufactures, and commerce of this country thirty or forty years ago formed but a very insignificant portion of the knowledge, wealth, influence, or population of the Empire.

Prior to that period, Britain was essentially agricultural. But, from that time to the present, the home and foreign trade have increased in a manner so rapid and extraordinary as to have raised commerce to an importance, which it never previously attained in any country possessing so much political power and influence.

(By the returns to the Population Act in 1811, it appears that in England, Scotland and Wales there are 895,998 families chiefly employed in agriculture—1,129,049 families chiefly employed in trade and manufactures—640,500 individuals in the army and navy—and 519,168 families not engaged in any of these employments. It follows that nearly half as many more persons are engaged in trade as in agriculture—and that of the whole population the agriculturalists are about 1 to 3.)

This change has been owing chiefly to the mechanical inventions which introduced the cotton trade into this country, and to the cultivation of the cotton tree in America. The wants which this trade created for the various materials requisite to forward its multiplied operations, caused an extraordinary demand for almost all the manufactures previously established, and, of course, for human labour. The numerous fanciful and useful fabrics manufactured from cotton soon became objects of desire in Europe and America: and the consequent extension of the British foreign trade was such as to astonish and confound the most enlightened statesmen both at home and abroad.

The general diffusion of manufactures throughout a country generates a new character in its inhabitants; and as this character is formed upon a principle quite unfavourable to individual or general happiness, it will produce the most lamentable and permanent evils, unless its tendency be counteracted by legislative interference and direction.

The manufacturing system has already so far extended its influence over the British Empire, as to effect an essential change in the general character of the mass of the people. This alteration is still in rapid progress; and ere long, the comparatively happy simplicity of the agricultural peasant will be wholly lost amongst us. It is even now scarcely anywhere to be found without a mixture of those habits which are the offspring of trade, manufactures, and commerce.

The acquisition of wealth, and the desire which it naturally creates for a continued increase, have introduced a fondness for essentially injurious luxuries among a numerous class of individuals who formerly never thought of them, and they have also generated a disposition which strongly impels its possessors to sacrifice the best feelings of human nature to this love of accumulation. To succeed in this career, the industry of the lower orders, from whose labour this wealth is now drawn, has been carried by new competitors striving against those of longer standing, to a point of real oppression reducing them by successive changes, as the spirit of competition increased and the ease of acquiring wealth diminished, to a state more wretched than can be imagined by those who have not attentively observed the changes as they have gradually occurred. In consequence, they are at present in a situation infinitely more degraded and miserable than they were before the introduction of these manufactories upon the success of which their bare subsistence now depends.

... Man so circumstanced sees all around him hurrying forward, at a mail-coach speed, to acquire individual wealth, regardless of him, his comforts, his wants, or even his sufferings, except by way of a *degrading parish charity*, fitted only to steel the heart of man against his fellows, or to form the tyrant and the slave. To-day he labours for one master, to-morrow for a second, then for a third, and a fourth, until all ties between employers and employed are frittered down to the consideration of what immediate gain each can derive from the other.

The employer regards the employed as mere instruments of gain, while these acquire a gross ferocity of character, which, if legislative measures shall not be judiciously devised to prevent its increase, and ameliorate the condition of this class, will sooner or later plunge the country into a formidable and perhaps inextricable state of danger.

Post-War Agitation

DOCUMENT 128

Samuel Bamford, Passages in the Life of a Radical (1840)

It is a matter of history, that whilst the laurels were yet cool on the brows of our victorious soldiers on their second occupation of Paris, the elements of convulsion were at work amongst the masses of our labouring population; and that a series of disturbances commenced with the introduction of the Corn Bill in 1815, and continued with short intervals, until the close of the year 1816. In London and Westminster riots ensued, and were continued for several days, whilst the bill was discussed: at Bridgeport there were riots on account of the high price of bread; at Biddeford there were similar disturbances to prevent the exportation of Grain; at Bury, by the unemployed, to destroy machinery; at Ely, not suppressed without bloodshed; at Newcastle-on-Tyne, by colliers and others; at Glasgow, where blood was shed, on account of the soup kitchens; at Preston by unemployed weavers; at Nottingham, by Luddites, who destroyed thirty frames; at Merthyr Tydville, on a reduction of wages; at Birmingham by the unemployed; at Walsall, by the distressed; and December 7th, 1816, at Dundee, where, owing to the high price of meal, upwards of one hundred shops were plundered. At this time the writings of William Cobbett suddenly became of great authority; they were read on nearly every cottage hearth in the manufacturing districts of South Lancashire; in those of Leicester, Derby and Nottingham; also in many of the Scottish manufacturing towns. Their influence was speedily visible; he directed his readers to the true cause of their sufferings—misgovernment; and to its proper corrective—parliamentary reform. Riots soon became scarce, and from that time they have never obtained their ancient vogue with the labourers of this country.

My Master and I
Quoted in The Common Muse

> Says the master to me, is it true? I am told
> Your name on the books of the Union's enroll'd,
> I can never allow that a workman of mine
> With wicked disturbers of peace should combine.
>
> Says I to the master, it's perfectly true
> That I am in the Union, and I'll stick to it too,
> And if between Union and you I must choose
> I have plenty to win and little to lose.
>
> For twenty years mostly my bread has been dry,
> And to butter it now I shall certainly try;
> And tho' I respect you, remember I'm free,
> No master in England shall trample on me.
>
> Says the master to me, a word or two more,
> We never have quarelled on matters before,
> If you stick to the Union, ere long I'll be bound,
> You will come and ask me for more wages all round.
>
> Now I cannot afford more than two bob a day
> When I look at the taxes and rent that I pay,
> And the crops are so injured by game as you see,
> If it is hard for you it's hard also for me.
>
> Says I to the master I do not see how
> Any need has arisen for quarrelling now,
> And tho' likely enough we shall ask for more wage
> I can promise you we shall not get first in a rage.

The Necessity of Unions

Rules and Orders to be observed by the Silk Weavers of Macclesfield, 20.2.1826
Quoted in A History of Macclesfield, ed. C. S. Davies, p. 190

Brother Tradesmen

If there were none but honest men in the world:—If men always acted upon the principles of justice and truth, and did unto others as they would others should do unto them, there would be no necessity for men to unite for their common protection and support; but since this is not the case and there are Manufacturers, who, if it were not for the liberal examples of others and being in some measure compelled by their servants, would never give what might be termed a fair price for their work—In this case it becomes necessary that we should unite, in order to keep these men up to the legal prices of the town—But this is not all, we have our trade to guard . . . moreover, a correspondence has been entered into with London and other places and a share has been obtained in the Trades Newspaper: for these and other reasons . . . it is absolutely necessary to form ourselves into a Union. . . . It must indeed be granted that there has been attempts of this sort before and have failed, but now let us try another plan. . . .

<h2 style="text-align:center">DOCUMENT 131</h2>

The Jubilee Volume of the London Society of Compositors 1898
Address issued by the Committee of the General Trade Society of Compositors
of London, 1st May 1833
Quoted in Cole and Filson, British Working Class Movements, p 244

To those who are ignorant of the proceedings of the London General Trade Society from its establishment in 1826 to the present period (1833) it is considered advisable to state that, since its commencement, not one member has quitted it on account of its mismanagement, its tardiness, inefficiency, or illiberality—its numbers have always been increasing—its receipts have been augmenting every year, and never has it been found necessary to withdraw its money from the public funds, although it has always paid its full proportion of all trade expenses, and has invariably been the foremost to reward those who have been injured in their attempts to maintain the rights of the trade.

The proceedings of the Society are openly conducted—no secret and partial investigations—no party decisions have ever stained its records—no wasteful expenditure or embezzlement of its receipts can ever take place—its accounts are publicly audited every quarter—its acts, its funds, its laws, are under the control of its members, who can at all times investigate or take part in the direction of its affairs. Its constitution is at once so simple and vigorous, yet so admirably framed to meet every circumstance that may arise, that it is enabled to afford the best advice in all cases of dispute with employers; it gives the most prompt assistance to all who need it—no tedious delays, no useless formalities fetter its proceedings, but it grants to its members immediate pecuniary aid and legal assistance, whenever such support and advice are required.

Since, then, it must be admitted by all, that those who live by their labour ought to unite to secure to themselves the just wages of labour, and since experience has shown that the disposition of masters in general is to grant the lowest possible remuneration for labour; and knowing, also, that without union amongst men, it is always in the power of employers to deprive

their workmen of even a proper share of the common necessaries of life—
it is a duty which every man owes to himself and to his family, to take such
steps as shall secure to him the proper reward of his industry. This just
reward, however, cannot be obtained by individual exertion—it is union
alone that can effect it. The only security to the workman from injustice,
oppression, and pauperism, is a well-conducted Trade Society; . . .

. . . It is only considered necessary, in conclusion, to remark that the
efficiency of the London General Trade Society is not weakened by a
variety of objects and a diversity of interests—it is truly a Trade Society,
since it has but one object in view—namely, the protection of the wages of
labour; and those who desire to reap the just reward of their industry, to
correct the evils arising from the illiberality and avarice of selfish employers,
and secure for themselves a never-failing shelter from powerful and wealthy
disputants, should, without further delay, enrol their names on the list of its
members.

DOCUMENT 132

Illustrated London News, August 1842

THE DISTURBANCES IN THE MANUFACTURING DISTRICTS

We have (August 1842) to record the disastrous occurrence of a turn-out
of manufacturing labourers in and about Manchester, which must be regarded with sorrow by wise and thoughtful men. It would appear that the
sudden and turbulent display of congregated thousands, leaving their daily
employment—marching upon mills, forcing willing and unwilling alike
to join them and, in a moment, paralysing the whole activity of the natural
enterprise of their neighbourhood,—arose, in the first instance, from a
reduction of wages in one quarter, given almost without notice, and taken
by the men as the omen of a general intention on the part of the masters
everywhere else. At once, with a desperation of purpose, they gathered in
half-starved thousands, resolved to abjure work, unless they can have 'a
fair day's pay for a fair day's labour'; and partly with riot, partly with invective, partly with threat, plunged the sober population into fear, and
created anxieties, natural to these troublous times, from one end to the other
of the land.

All the manufacturing districts have been up in arms; at Preston the
insurgents were fired upon, and some of them wounded mortally. At
Stockport, where there are upwards of 20,000 persons out of employment
who have no resources but those of plunder and beggary, a large body of
rioters broke open and pillaged the workhouses of food and clothing, and
mobs robbed the provision shops. Troops, guards, and artillery have been
poured in upon the shocking scene of insurrection; and there seems to have
been a spreading organisation of a most formidable and disciplined character.
The fact that troops had been ordered off to the disturbed districts soon

became publicly known, and produced an intense feeling of alarm and excitement in the mind of individuals generally.

The anti-corn-law leaguer and the chartist are, we fear, responsible for these agitations—responsible, as we think, to their Queen, their country, and their God. We are no partisans; we do not oppose, abstractedly for their peculiar doctrines, either the chartist or the anti-corn-law leaguer; we leave all political opinion, however violent, its fair play; but we despise the infamous diplomacy which would make its game out of the miseries of the people. Nothing can more excite our indignant rebuke than the revolutionary villain or the quack preacher of politics, who says, 'I have a charter to achieve here, or a corn-law to repeal there, and, now that the people are starving and in tatters, I will convert their rags into banners of rebellion, and their hunger into the sign of blood.' Yet this, we believe, is the course that was pursued, furnishing the key to all the riots and seditions that disturbed the land.

Every way we lament the dismal occurrences that have transpired, from which, because they are destitute of social peace and order, even the justification of injury is taken away. Heaven knows that our cause is with the poor, and strongly have we reasoned and remonstrated on their behalf; but we set up JUSTICE and HUMANITY as our household gods, and for neither rich nor poor will we despoil their altars. There is no justice, there is no humanity, in the late revolts; and although we rest their blame and guilt more upon the inciters that the enactors of the crime, yet we will not take the part of the latter because we execrate the former.

FURTHER PARTICULARS OF THE DISTURBANCES

Reports stated that immense bodies of rioters from Wigan, Chorley, and the district of the collieries, some making them as numerous as 15,000, armed with axes, spades, bludgeons, etc. were on their way to Preston. It was reported that a large cotton factory at Bamberbridge was partially destroyed by the mob. From the church steeple and the North Union Railway bridge, which commanded extensive views of the various roads to Preston, it was soon ascertained that the mob were in a body on their road towards the town of Chorley. However, the police and military were all brought together, and took up their station near Walton-bridge, the police being in the turnpike road, and the Rifles on each side concealed behind the hedges. About three o'clock in the afternoon a mob of about 1,000 persons, chiefly armed with iron truncheons, reached Walton, passed through the village, and were about entering the town, when the police force attempted to prevent them, and in consequence a battle commenced. Several of the police were severely wounded, one of whom had two fingers nearly severed from his hand by a blow with an iron bar. It soon became evident that the police force would be defeated, and the appearance of the mob became so alarming that orders were given to the military, who instantly burst through the hedges on each side of the road, and presented a bold front to the mob. The sudden appearance of the Rifles spread consternation and dismay in the ranks of the insurgents, who fled in all directions.

The more remarkable features of the proceedings at Stockport were the extortion of money from mill-owners as well as shopkeepers, and an attack on the New Union Workhouse, Shaw-heath, where the mob forced an entrance and immediately commenced to help themselves to bread and money. Information of this was conveyed to the authorities, and they hastened to the spot with the constables, and infantry, and captured about forty of the rioteers.

Men v Masters

DOCUMENT 133

Mrs Gaskell, Mary Barton (1848)

I am not sure if I can express myself in the technical terms of either masters or workmen, but I will try simply to state the case on which the latter deliberated.

An order for coarse goods came in from a new foreign market. It was a large order, giving employment to all the mills engaged in that species of manufacture; but it was necessary to execute it speedily, and at as low prices as possible, as the masters had reason to believe that a duplicate order had been sent to one of the continental manufacturing towns, where there were no restrictions on food, no taxes on building or machinery, and where consequently they dreaded that the goods could be made at a much lower price than they could afford them for; and that, by so acting and charging, the rival manufacturers would obtain undivided possession of the market. It was clearly their interest to buy cotton as cheaply, and to beat down wages as low as possible. And in the long run the interests of the workmen would have been thereby benefited. Distrust each other as they may, the employers and the employed must rise or fall together. There may be some difference as to chronology, none as to fact.

But the masters did not choose to make all these circumstances known. They stood upon being the masters, and that they had a right to order work at their own prices, and they believed that in the present depression of trade, and unemployment of hands, there would be no great difficulty in getting it done.

Now let us turn to the workmen's view of the question. The masters (of the tottering foundation of whose prosperity they were ignorant) seemed doing well, and, like gentlemen, 'lived at home in ease', while they were starving, gasping on from day to day; and there was a foreign order to be executed, the extent of which, large as it was, was greatly exaggerated; and it was to be done speedily. Why were the masters offering such low wages under these circumstances? Shame upon them! It was taking advantage of their work-people being almost starved; but they would starve entirely rather than come in to such terms. It was bad enough to be poor, while the labour of their hands, the sweat of their brows, the masters were made rich; but they would not be utterly ground down to dust. No! They would fold their hands and sit idle, and smile at the masters, whom even in death they could baffle. With Spartan endurance they determined to let the employers know their power, by refusing to work.

So class distrusted class, and their want of mutual confidence wrought sorrow to both. The masters would not be bullied, and compelled to reveal why they felt it wisest and best to offer only such low wages; they would not be made to tell that they were even sacrificing capital to obtain a decisive victory over the continental manufacturers. And the workmen sat silent and stern with folded hands refusing to work for such pay. There was a strike in Manchester.

Of course it was succeeded by the usual consequences. Many other Trades' Unions, connected with different branches of business, supported with money, countenance and encouragement of every kind, the stand which the Manchester power-loom weavers were making against their masters. Delegates from Glasgow, from Nottingham, and other towns, were sent to Manchester, to keep up the spirit of resistance, a committee was formed, and all the requisite officers elected; chairman, treasurer, honorary secretary.

The masters, meanwhile, took their measure. They placarded the walls with advertisements for power-loom weavers. The workmen replied with a placard in still larger letters, stating their grievances. The masters met daily in town, to mourn over the time (so fast slipping away) for the fulfilment of the foreign orders; and to strengthen each other in their resolution not to yield. If they gave up now, they might give up always. It would never do. And amongst the most energetic of the masters, the Carsons, father and son, took their places. It is well known, that there is no religionist so zealous as a convert; no master so stern, and regardless of the interests of their work-people, as those who have risen from such a station themselves. This would account for the elder Mr Carson's determination not to be bullied into yielding; not even to be bullied into giving reasons for acting as the masters did. It was the employers' will, and that should be enough for the employed.

Meanwhile, the power-loom weavers living in the more remote parts of Lancashire, and the neighbouring counties, heard of the masters' advertise-ments for workmen; and in their solitary dwellings grew weary of starvation, and resolved to come to Manchester. Foot-sore, wayworn, half-starved-looking men they were, as they tried to steal into town in the early dawn, before people were astir, or in the dusk of the evening. And now began the real wrongdoings of the Trades' Unions. As to their decision to work, or not, at such a particular rate of wages, that was either wise or unwise; all error of judgment at the worst. But they had no right to tyrannise over others, and tie them down to their own Procrustean bed. Abhorring what they considered oppression in the masters, why did they oppress others? Because, when men get excited, they know not what they do.

In spite of policemen, set to watch over the safety of the poor country weavers—in spite of magistrates and prisons, and severe punishments—the poor depressed men tramping in from Burnley, Padiham, and other places, to work at the condemned 'Starvation Prices', were waylaid, and beaten. and left by the roadside, almost for dead. The police broke up every lounging knot of men—they separated quietly, to reunite half-a-mile out of town.

Of course the feeling between the masters and workmen did not improve under these circumstances.

Combination is an awful power. It is like the equally mighty agency of steam; capable of almost unlimited good or evil. But to obtain a blessing on its labours, it must work under the direction of a high and intelligent will; incapable of being misled by passion or excitement. The will of the operatives had not been guided by the calmness of wisdom.

Co-operation

DOCUMENT 134

William Lovett, Life and Struggles, pp 41–2

The members subscribed a small weekly sum for the raising of a common fund, with which they opened a general store, containing such articles of food, clothing, books, etc. as were most in request among workmen; the profits of which were added to the common stock. As their fund increased some of them employed their members; such as shoemakers, tailors, and other domestic trades: paying them journeyman's wages, and adding the profits to their funds. Many of them were also enabled by these means to raise sufficient capital to commence manufactures on a small scale; such as broadcloth, silk, linen, worsted goods, shoes, hats, cutlery, furniture, etc.

The Health of the Nation

Effects of Factory Labour

The accelerating pace of economic growth in early nineteenth-century Britain was not achieved by technological progress alone and the exploitation of the new factory labour force was physical, as well as financial. Hard work had always brought occupational diseases in the past, but their extent and severity seem to have been enlarged by the conditions of factory labour. We must, however, remember that the evidence we have for this is very partisan, and, therefore, to be accepted with reservations. Nevertheless, the new pace of labour seems not only to have produced more than its fair share of cripples and invalids, but also to have contributed to a more general weakening of the constitutions of the urban workers, who were thus an easier prey for the ravages of epidemic disease.

DOCUMENT 135

Resolutions for the consideration of the Manchester Board of Health by Dr Percival, 25th January 1796—reprinted in Report of Peel's Committee H.C. 1816, III, p 377
Quoted in B. L. Hutchins and A. Harrison, A History of Factory Legislation

It has already been stated that the objects of the present institution are to prevent the generation of diseases; to obviate the spreading of them by contagion, and to shorten the duration of those which exist, by affording the necessary aids and comforts to the sick. In the prosecution of this interesting undertaking, the Board have had their attention particularly directed to the large cotton factories established in the town and neighbourhood of Manchester; and they feel it a duty incumbent on them to lay before the public the result of their enquiries:

1. It appears that the children and others who work in the large cotton factories, are peculiarly disposed to be affected by the contagion of fever, and that when such infection is received, it is rapidly propagated, not only amongst those who are crowded together in the same apartments, but in the families and neighbourhoods to which they belong.

2. The large factories are generally injurious to the constitution of those

employed in them, even where no particular diseases prevail, from the debilitating effects of hot and impure air, and from the want of the active exercises which nature points out as essential in childhood and youth to invigorate the system, and to fit our species for the employments and for the duties of manhood.

3. The untimely labour of the night, and the protracted labour of the day, with respect to children, not only tends to diminish future expectations as to the general sum of life and industry, by impairing the strength and destroying the vital stamina of the rising generation, but it too often gives encouragement to idleness, extravagance and profligacy in the parents, who, contrary to the order of nature, subsist by the oppression of their offspring.

4. It appears that the children employed in factories are generally debarred from all opportunities of education, and from moral or religious instruction.

5. From the excellent regulations which subsist in several cotton factories, it appears that many of these evils may be in a considerable degree obviated; we are therefore warranted by experience, and are assured we shall have the support of the liberal proprietors of these factories in proposing an application for parliamentary aid (if other methods appear not likely to effect the purpose) to establish a general syetem of laws for the wise, humane and equal government of all such works.

DOCUMENT 136

P. Gaskell, The Manufacturing Population of England (1833), Ch 4

The vast deterioration in personal form which has been brought about in the manufacturing population, during the last thirty years, a period not extending over one generation, is singularly impressive, and fills the mind with contemplations of a very painful character. . . .

Any man who has stood at twelve o'clock at the single narrow doorway, which serves as the place of exit for the hands employed in the great cotton-mills, must acknowledge that an uglier set of men and women, of boys and girls, taken in the mass, it would be impossible to congregate in a smaller compass. Their complexion is sallow and pallid—with a peculiar flatness of feature, caused by the want of a proper quantity of adipose substance to cushion out the cheeks. Their stature low—the average height of four hundred men, measured at different times, and at different places, being five feet six inches. Their limbs slender, and playing badly and ungracefully. A very general bowing of the legs. Great numbers of girls and women walking lamely or awkwardly, with raised chests and spinal flexures. Nearly all have flat feet, accompanied with a down-tread, differing very widely from the elasticity of action in the foot and ankle, attendant upon perfect formation. Hair thin and straight—many of the men having but little beard, and that in patches of a few hairs, much resembling its growth among the red men of America. A spiritless and dejected air, a sprawling and wide action of the legs, and an appearance, taken as a whole, giving the world but 'little assurance of a man', or if so, 'most sadly cheated of his fair proportions'.

A Contrary Opinion

DOCUMENT 137

Rickman, Directory of the Census (1816) to the poet Southey
Quoted in M. D. George, England in Transition, p. 76

One thing I wish to say as to an opinion you entertain as to the well-being or rather ill-being of the poor, that their state has grown worse and worse of late. Now, if one listens to common assertion, everything in grumbling England grows worse and worse; but the fact in question is even a curiosity. Human comfort is to be estimated by human health, and that by the length of human life. . . . Since 1780 life has been prolonged by 5 to 4—and the poor form too large a portion of society to be excluded from this general effect; rather they are the main cause of it; for the upper classes had food and cleanliness abundant before.

The Urban Explosion

DOCUMENT 138

Report of Select Committee on the Health of Towns, PP 1840, vol XI,
pp iii–ix

By reference to the Population Returns it appears that, from the beginning of the present century, the whole population of Great Britain has increased at the rate of nearly 16 per cent every ten years; from 1801 to 1811, thence to 1821, and again to 1831; and there is every reason to believe about the same rate of increase will be found to have taken place next year, when the next decennial return will be made. Whilst, however, such has been the increase in the population of the kingdom at large, reference to the same returns shows, that the augmentation of numbers in the great towns of the realm has been much more rapid: thus, whilst the increase of population in England and Wales, in thirty years, from 1801 to 1831, has been something more than 47 per cent, the actual increase in the number of inhabitants of five of our most important provincial towns has very nearly doubled that rate; being Manchester 109 per cent, Glasgow 108 per cent, Birmingham, 73 per cent, Leeds 99 per cent, Liverpool 100 per cent, giving an average increase of almost 98 per cent in five cities, whose united population in 1831 amounted to 844,700, and at the present time may be calculated at not less than 1,126,000. Far the larger portion of this vast body of persons are engaged constantly in occupations connected with manufactures or commerce. . . .

Your Committee do not wish to go here into details as to the miserable and neglected state of the dwellings of the poorer classes in various districts of the metropolis and other large towns, but refer to the evidence . . . in which statements of the most melancholy and appalling nature will be found. It will there be seen, that the sewerage, draining, and cleansing is (in many places inhabited by dense masses of the working classes) greatly neglected; that the most necessary precautions to preserve their health in many cases appears to have been forgotten; that in consequence fevers and other disorders of a contagious and fatal nature are shown to prevail to a very alarming extent, causing widespread misery among the families of the sufferers, often entailing weakness and prostration of strength among the survivors; and becoming the source of great expense to the parishes and more opulent classes. . . .

Your Committee would observe, that it is painful to contemplate, in the midst of what appears to be an opulent, spirited, and flourishing community, such a vast multitude of our poorer fellow subjects, the instruments by whose hands these riches were created, condemned, for no fault of their own, to the evils so justly complained of, and placed in situations where it is almost impracticable for them to preserve health or decency of deportment, or to keep themselves and their children from moral and physical contamination; to require them to be clean, sober, cheerful, contented, under such circumstances would be a vain and unreasonable expectation. There is no Building Act to enforce the dwellings of these workmen being properly constructed; no draining Act to enforce their being efficiently drained; no general or local regulations to enforce the commonest provisions for cleanliness and comfort.

It appears to Your Committee . . . that where such evils are found to follow from the neglect or inability in these respects of local authorities, that it is the duty of the Legislature to take efficient steps to protect so numerous and valuable a portion of the community. . . .

Cellar Dwelling—Housing in Stockton

DOCUMENT 139

Report on the Sanitary Condition of the Labouring Population (1842),
pp 17–18

Shepherd's Buildings consist of two rows of houses with a street seven yards wide between them; each row consists of what are styled back and front houses—that is two houses placed back to back. There are no yards or out-conveniences; the privies are in the centre of each row, about a yard wide; over them there is part of a sleeping-room; there is no ventilation in the bedrooms; each house contains two rooms, viz., a house place and sleeping room above; each room is about three yards wide and four long. In one of these houses there are nine persons belonging to one family, and the mother on the eve of her confinement. There are 44 houses in the two rows, and 22 cellars, all of the same size. The cellars are let off as separate dwellings; these are dark, damp, and very low, not more than six feet between the ceiling and floor. The street between the two rows is seven yards wide, in the centre of which is the common gutter, or more properly sink, into which all sorts of refuse are thrown; it is a foot in depth. Thus there is always a quantity of putrefying matter contaminating the air. At the end of the rows is a pool of water very shallow and stagnant, and a few yards further, a part of the town's gas works. In many of these dwellings there are four persons in one bed.

Housing Conditions of the Factory Workers

DOCUMENT 140

Report on the Sanitary Condition of the Labouring Population: Lords Sessional Reports (1842), vol 26, p 239

On the early introduction of the cotton manufacture, the parties who entered into it were often men of limited capital, and anxious to invest the whole of it in mills and machinery, and therefore too much absorbed with the doubtful success of their own affairs to look after the necessities of their workpeople.

Families were attracted from all parts for the benefit of employment, and obliged as a temporary resort to crowd together into such dwellings as the neighbourhood afforded: often two families into one house; others into cellars or very small dwellings; eventually, as the works became established, either the proprietor or some neighbour would probably see it advantageous to build a few cottages; these were often of the worst description: in such case the prevailing consideration was not how to promote the health and comfort of the occupants, but how many cottages could be built upon the smallest space of ground and at the least possible cost.

Whatever the weekly income, the wife could never make such a house comfortable; she had only one room in which to do all her work; it may be readily supposed the husband would not always find the comfort he wished in such a home. The public-house would then be his only resort; But here the evil does not end; the children brought up in such dwellings knew no better accommodation than such afforded, nor had they any opportunities of seeing better domestic arrangements.

DOCUMENT 141

Engels, The Condition of the Working Class in England in 1844, p 48

... First of all, there is the old town of Manchester, which lies between the northern boundary of the commercial district and the Irk. Here the streets, even the better ones, are narrow and winding, as Todd Street, Long Millgate, Withy Grove, and Shude Hill, the houses dirty, old, and tumble-down, and the construction of the side streets utterly horrible. Going from the Old Church to Long Millgate, the stroller has at once a row of old-fashioned houses at the right, of which not one has kept its original level; these are remnants of the old pre-manufacturing Manchester, whose former inhabitants have removed with their descendants into better-built districts, and have left the houses, which were not good enough for them, to a population strongly mixed with Irish blood. Here one is in an almost undisguised working-men's quarter, for even the shops and beerhouses hardly take the trouble to exhibit a trifling degree of cleanliness. But all this is nothing in comparison with the courts and lanes which lie behind, to which access can be gained only through covered passages, in which no two human beings can pass at the same time. Of the irregular cramming together of dwellings in ways which defy all rational plan, of the tangle in which they are crowded literally one upon the other, it is impossible to convey an idea. And it is not the buildings surviving from the old times of Manchester which are to blame for this; the confusion has only recently reached its height when every scrap of space left by the old way of building has been filled up and patched over until not a foot of land is left to be further occupied.

Privations and Death

DOCUMENT 142

S. R. Bosanquet, The Rights of the Poor and Christian Almsgiving Vindicated (1841), pp 51–2, quoting Howard 'The Morbid Effects of Deficiency of Food'

The public generally have a very inadequate idea of the number of persons who perish annually from deficiency of food. . . . Although death directly produced by hunger may be rare, there can be no doubt that a very large proportion of the mortality amongst the labouring classes is attributable to deficiency of food as a main cause, aided by too long continued toil and exertion without adequate repose, insufficient clothing exposure to cold and other privations to which the poor are subjected.

The mid-Victorian campaign for 'sanitary reform' implies a new consciousness of the economic and social significance of disease and, more fundamentally, a new belief that effective action could be taken to prevent its outbreak or minimise its consequences. Disease had been accepted as natural and inevitable in pre-industrial England. What industrialisation achieved was to cram large numbers of people in substandard housing, in sprawling agglomerations, without adequate supplies of fresh water or means of sewage disposal. Disease found an ideal breeding ground and appeared in new and terrifying forms, like cholera, which claimed thousands of victims suddenly and arbitrarily attacking the prosperous as well as the labouring classes.

The vigorous movement for sanitary reform derived its impetus from the efforts of Edwin Chadwick, more than any other single man, though Southwood Smith, Kay-Shuttleworth and Simon all played important, if less spectacular, roles. Chadwick, a zealous disciple of the rationalist philosopher Bentham, was originally concerned with the administration of the reformed Poor Law of 1834, an interest which led him to involve himself in the novel procedure of registering births, deaths and marriages, which began in 1837. Chadwick ordered that cause of death be recorded wherever possible and thus compiled the first set of comprehensive statistics on which rational debate about disease could be based. For Chadwick the most significant feature to emerge was the apparently close connection between death from water-borne disease and high poor rates. He came to convince himself that investment in water supplies and sewerage systems could more than pay for itself in the long run by the saving it would bring in poor rates, as wage-earners would no longer be cut off in their prime and leave a family for the community to support. Chadwick's massive propagandist 'Report on the Sanitary Condition of the Labouring Population' (1842), coupled with an outbreak of cholera, led to the passing of the first Public Health Act in 1848. The Board of Health which it set up did some good work before it was dissolved in 1854 but the campaign for sanitary reform was hampered by fatalistic prejudice, rate-payers' preference for 'cheap government', distrust of state intervention and the problem of urban property rights. General success did not become apparent until the 1870s when death-rates finally began a long decline to their present level.

DOCUMENT 143

*Report on the Sanitary Condition of the Labouring Population (1842)
Quoted in E. N. Williams, A Documentary History of England (1559–1931)*

After as careful an examination of the evidence collected as I have been enabled to make, I beg leave to recapitulate the chief conclusions which that evidence appears to me to establish.

First, as to the extent and operation of the evils which are the subject of the inquiry:

That the various forms of epidemic, endemic, and other disease caused, or aggravated, or propagated chiefly amongst the labouring classes by atmospheric impurities produced by decomposing animal and vegetable substances, by damp and filth, and close and overcrowded dwellings prevail amongst the population in every part of the kingdom, whether dwelling in separate houses, in rural villages, in small towns, in the larger towns— as they have been found to prevail in the lowest districts of the metropolis.

That such disease, wherever its attacks are frequent, is always found in connexion with the physical circumstances above specified, and that where those circumstances are removed by drainage, proper cleansing, better ventilation, and other means of diminishing atmospheric impurity, the frequency and intensity of such disease is abated; and where the removal of the noxious agencies appears to be complete, such disease almost entirely disappears.

That high prosperity in respect to employment and wages, and various and abundant food, have afforded to the labouring classes no exemptions from attacks of epidemic disease, which have been as frequent and as fatal in periods of commercial and manufacturing prosperity as in any others.

That the formation of all habits of cleanliness is obstructed by defective supplies of water.

That the annual loss of life from filth and bad ventilation are greater than the loss from death or wounds in any wars in which the country has been engaged in modern times.

That of the 43,000 cases of widowhood, and 112,000 cases of destitute orphanage relieved from the poor's rates in England and Wales alone, it appears that the greastest proportion of deaths of the heads of families occurred from the above specified and other removable causes; that their ages were under 45 years; that is to say, 13 years below the natural probabilities of life as shown by the experience of the whole population of Sweden.

That the public loss from the premature deaths of the heads of families is greater than can be that represented by any enumeration of the pecuniary burdens consequent upon their sickness and death.

That, measuring the loss of working ability amongst large classes by the instances of gain, even from incomplete arrangements for the removal of noxious influences from places of work or from abodes, that this loss cannot be less than eight or ten years.

That the ravages of epidemics and other diseases do not diminish but tend to increase the pressure of population.

That in the districts where the mortality is the greatest the births are not only sufficient to replace the numbers removed by death, but to add to the population.

That the younger population, bred up under noxious physical agencies, is inferior in physical organisation and general health to a population preserved from the presence of such agencies.

That the population so exposed is less susceptible of moral influences, and the effects of education are more transient than with a healthy population.

That these adverse circumstances tend to produce an adult population short lived, improvident, reckless, and intemperate, and with habitual avidity for sensual gratifications.

That these habits lead to the abandonment of all the conveniences and decencies of life, and especially lead to the overcrowding of homes, which is destructive to morality as well as the health of large classes of both sexes.

That defective town cleansing fosters habits of the most abject degradation and tends to the demoralisation of large numbers of human beings, who subsist by means of what they find amidst the noxious filth accumulated in neglected streets and bye-places.

That the expenses of local public works are in general unequally and unfairly assessed, oppressively and uneconomically collected, by separate collections, wastefully expended in separate and inefficient operations by unskilled and practically irresponsible officers.

That the existing law for the protection of the public health and the constitutional machinery for reclaiming its execution, such as the Courts Leet, have fallen into desuetude, and are in the state indicated by the prevalence of the evils they were intended to prevent.

Secondly, as to the means by which the present sanitary condition of the labouring classes may be improved:

The primary and most important measures, and at the same time the most practicable, and within the recognised province of public administration, are drainage, the removal of all refuse of habitations, streets, and roads, and the improvement of the supplies of water.

That the chief obstacles to the immediate removal of decomposing refuse of towns and habitations have been the expense and annoyance of the hand labour and cartage requisite for the purpose.

That this expense may be reduced to one-twentieth or to one-thirtieth, or rendered inconsiderable, by the use of water and self-acting means of removal by improved and cheaper sewers and drains.

That refuse when thus held in suspension in water may be most cheaply and innoxiously conveyed to any distance out of towns, and also in the best form for productive use, and that the loss and injury by the pollution of natural streams may be avoided.

That for all these purposes, as well as for domestic use, better supplies of water are absolutely necessary.

That for successful and economical drainage the adoption of geological areas as the basis of operations is requisite.

That appropriate scientific arrangements for public drainage would afford important facilities for private land-drainage, which is important for the health as well as sustenance of the labouring classes.

That the expense of public drainage, of supplies of water laid on in houses, and of means of improved cleansing would be a pecuniary gain, by diminishing the existing charges attendant on sickness and premature mortality.

That for the protection of the labouring classes and of the ratepayers against inefficiency and waste in all new structural arrangements for the protection of the public health, and to ensure public confidence that the expenditure will be beneficial, securities should be taken that all new local public works are devised and conducted by responsible officers qualified by the possession of the science and skill of civil engineers.

That the oppressiveness and injustices of levies for the whole immediate outlay on such works upon persons who have only short interests in the benefits may be avoided by care in spreading the expense over periods coincident with the benefits.

That by appropriate arrangements, 10 or 15 per cent on the ordinary outlay for drainage might be saved, which on an estimate of the expense of the necessary structural alterations of one-third only of the existing tenements would be a saving of one million and a half sterling, besides the reduction of the future expenses of management.

That for the prevention of the disease occasioned by defective ventilation, and other causes of impurity in places of work and other places where large numbers are assembled, and for the general promotion of the means necessary to prevent disease, that it would be good economy to appoint a district medical officer independent of private practice, and with the securities of special qualifications and responsibilities, to initiate sanitary measures and reclaim the execution of the law.

That by the combinations of all these arrangements, it is probable that the full ensurable period of life indicated by the Swedish tables; that is, an increase of 13 years at least, may be extended to the whole of the labouring classes.

That the attainment of these and the other collateral advantages of reducing existing charges and expenditure are within the power of legislature, and are dependent mainly on the securities taken for the application of practical science, skill and economy in the direction of local public works.

And that the removal of noxious physical circumstances, and the promotion of civic, household, and personal cleanliness, are necessary to the improvement of the moral condition of the population; for that sound morality and refinement in manners and health are not long found co-existent with filthy habits amongst any class of the community.

Population Growth and the Nation's Health

DOCUMENT 144

G. R. Porter, Progress of the Nation, pp 20–1

. . . a continually diminishing mortality. This effect, so strongly indicative of amendment in the condition of the people, must be attributed to the coincidence of various causes. Among these may be mentioned the less-crowded state of our dwellings; the command of better kinds of food; the superiority and cheapness of clothing; and probably, also, more temperate habits and greater personal cleanliness. One influential cause of the diminished rate of mortality will be found in the introduction of vaccination, which has had so powerful an effect in diminishing the rate of mortality among children; besides these, the extensive surface drainage which has been going forward in those parts of the country which, owing to the presence of stagnant waters, were once productive of intermittent fevers, has added to the general healthiness of the country.

Rural Society

Preface

Industrialisation stimulated the growth of existing towns and the creation of new ones; it also profoundly altered the structure of rural society beyond the towns. The term 'agricultural revolution' may be even more misleading than the historian's 'industrial revolution' but the term 'revolution' could certainly be applied to describe the extent of change which took place, if not the pace at which it occurred. Large areas of land were brought into cultivation and even larger areas changed ownership; new techniques of production created new occupations, while the rapid rise of rural population contributed more labour than the land could profitably employ, thus setting up severe social tensions within the village community. At the same time the high productivity of urban factories undermined rural crafts, destroying many part-time and seasonal opportunities to boost the labourer's slender income. New transport systems made contact with new markets and facilitated the migration of labour. The spread of literacy and the new ideas that went with it began to undermine the traditional authority of the squire and the parson. Urban values were translated into a rural context, but the process operated slowly and motor transport, television and radio have yet to complete what turnpike roads began.

DOCUMENT 145

Oliver Goldsmith, The Deserted Village (1770), lines 35, 64, 265–82, 303–8

> Sweet smiling village, loveliest of the lawn,
> Thy sports are fled, and all thy charms withdrawn;
> Amidst thy bowers the tyrant's hand is seen
> And desolation saddens all thy green.
> One only master grasps the whole domain,

And half a tillage stints thy smiling plain . . .
And trembling, shrinking from the spoiler's hand,
Far, far away, thy children leave the land . . .
Where then, ah! where shall poverty reside
To 'scape the pressure of continuous pride?
If to some common's fenceless limits strayed,
He drives his flock to pick the scanty blade,
Those fenceless fields the sons of wealth divide,
And e'en the bare-worn common is denied.
Ye friends to truth, ye statesmen who survey
The rich man's joys increase, the poor's decay,
'Tis yours to judge how wide the limits stand
Between a splendid and happy land . . .
Ill fares the land, to hastening ills a prey,
Where wealth accumulates, and men decay;
Princes and lords may flourish, or may fade;
A breath can make them, as a breath has made,
But a bold peasantry, their country's pride,
When once destroyed, can never be supplied.

Effects of Enclosure

DOCUMENT 146

*Rev. D. Davies, The Case of the Labourers in Husbandry (1795), pp 55–7
Quoted in G. D. H. Cole and A. W. Filson, British Working Class
Movements, Selected Documents 1789–1875*

The practice of enlarging and engrossing of farms, and especially that of
depriving the peasantry of all landed property, have contributed greatly
to increase the number of dependent poor.

The land-owner, to render his income adequate to the increased expense
of living, unites several small farms into one, raises the rent to the utmost,
and avoids the expense of repairs. The rich farmer also engrosses as many
farms as he is able to stock; lives in more credit and comfort than he could
otherwise do; and out of the profits of the *several farms*, makes an ample
provision for *one family*. Thus thousands of families, which formerly gained
an independent livelihood on those separate farms, have been gradually
reduced to the class of day-labourers. But day-labourers are sometimes
in want of work, and are sometimes unable to work; and in either case their
resort is the parish. It is a fact, that thousands of parishes have not now
half the number of farmers which they had formerly. And in proportion
as the number of farming families has decreased, the number of poor families
has increased.

Thus an amazing number of people have been reduced from a comfortable state of partial independence to the precarious conditions of hirelings, who, when out of work, must immediately come to their parish. And the great plenty of working hands always to be had when wanted, having kept down the price of labour below its proper level, the consequence is universally felt in the increased number of dependent poor.

The New Farmer

DOCUMENT 147

The Times Have Altered (c. *1820*)
Quoted in The Common Muse

Come all you swaggering farmers, whoever you may be,
One moment pay attention and listen unto me;
It is concerning former times, as I to you declare,
So different to the present times if you with them compare.

Chorus
For lofty heads and paltry pride, I'm sure it's all the go,
For to distress poor servants and keep their wages low.

If you'd seen the farmers wives 'bout fifty years ago,
In home-spun russet linsey clad from top to toe;
But now a-days the farmer's wives are so puffed up with pride,
In a dandy habit and green veil unto the market they must ride.

Some years ago the farmer's sons were learnt to plough and sow,
And when the summer-time did come, likewise to reap and mow;
But now they dress like Squire's sons, their pride it knows no bounds,
They mount upon a fine blood horse to follow up the hounds.

The farmer's daughters formerly were learnt to card and spin,
And, by their own industry, good husbands they did win;
But now the card and spinning-wheel are forced to take their chance,
While they're hopped off to a boarding-school to learn to sing and dance.

In a decent black silk bonnet to church they used to go,
Black shoes, and handsome cotton gown, stockings as white as snow,
But now silk gowns and coloured shoes they must be bought for them,
Besides they are frizzed and furbelowed just like a friezland hen.

Each morning when at breakfast, the master and the dame
Down with the servants they would sit, and eat and drink the same,
But with such good old things, they've done them quite away;
Into the parlour they do go with coffee, toast, and tea.

At the kitchen table formerly, the farmer he would sit,
And carve for all his servants, both pudding and fine meat,
But now all in the dining-room so closely they're boxed in,
If a servant only was to peep, it would be thought a sin.

Now, in those good old fashion'd times, the truth I do declare,
The rent and taxes could be spared, and money for to spare,
But now they keep the fashion up, they look so very nice,
Although they cut an outside show they are as poor as mice.

When Bonaparte was in vogue, poor servants could engage
For sixteen pounds a year, my boys, that was a handsome wage,
But now the wages are so low, and what is worse than all,
The masters cannot find the cash, which brings them to the wall.

When fifty acres they did rent, then money they could save,
But now for to support their pride, five hundred they must have;
If those great farms were taken and divided into ten,
Oh! we might see as happy days as ever we did then.

Farmers and Labourers

DOCUMENT 148

Cobbett, Political Register, 17th March 1821

I hold a return to small farms to be absolutely necessary to a restoration to
anything like an English community; and I am quite sure, that the ruin
of the present race of farmers, generally, is a necessary preliminary to this . . .
The life of the husbandman cannot be that of a *gentleman* without injury
to society at large. When farmers become *gentlemen* their labourers become
slaves. A *Virginian* farmer, as he is called, very much resembles a *great farmer*
in England; but then, the Virginian's work is done by slaves. It is in those
States of America, where the farmer is only the *first labourer* that all the
domestic virtues are to be found, and all that public spirit and that valour,
which are the safeguards of American independence, freedom, and happiness.
You, Sir, with others, complain of the increase of the *poor-rates*. But, you
seem to forget, that, in the destruction of the small farms, as separate farms,
small-farmers have become mere hired labourers. . . . Take England throughout, *three farms have been turned into one within fifty years*, and as far greater

part of the change has taken place within the last *thirty years*; that is to say, since the commencement of the deadly system of PITT. Instead of families of small farmers with all their exertions, all their decency of dress and of manners, and all their scrupulousness as to character, we have *families of paupers*, with all the improvidence and wrecklessness belonging to an irrevocable sentence of poverty for life. Mr CURWEN in his *Hints on Agriculture*, observes that he saw somewhere in Norfolk, I believe it was, *two hundred* farmers worth from *five to ten thousands pounds each*; and exclaims 'What a *glorious* sight!' In commenting on this passage in the Register, in the year 1810, I observed 'Mr CURWEN only saw the *outside* of the sepulchre; if he had seen the *two or three thousand* half-starved labourers of these two hundred farmers, and the *five or six thousand* ragged wives and children of those labourers; if the farmers had brought those with them, the sight would not have been so *glorious.*'

Rural Housing

DOCUMENT 149

The Quarterly Review, 1825
Quoted in English Historical Documents, Vol XI

... It is not many years ago that the cottages in the country had no flooring but that which nature furnished, and that a composition of lime and sand was beheld by the neighbours of him who enjoyed such a refinement, as a luxury to be envied. The mud walls were rarely covered with any coat of plastering; there was no ceiling under the straw roof, and when any chamber was in the house, it was accessible only by a ladder or by a post with notches indented to receive the foot in climbing to it. The doors and windows did not close sufficiently to exclude the rain or the snow, and in wet weather puddles were scattered over the inequalities in the mud floor. It is now rare in the country to see a cottage without a brick or stone or wood floor, without stairs to its chambers, without plastering on the walls, and without doors and windows tolerably weather-tight. The furniture and domestic utensils are increased and improved with the houses. The paucity and the homeliness which appeared forty or fifty years ago present to the recollection of those who can remember the state of that day, a striking contrast with the comparative abundance and convenience which are now exhibited. Instead of straw beds, and a single rug for a covering, are substituted feather or flock beds, several blankets, sheets, and often a cotton quilt. Chairs and tables occupy the place of benches and joint stools. Wooden trenchers have given way to earthenware plates and dishes, and to the iron pot is now commonly added the gridiron, frying-pan and saucepans. ...

The clothing of our poor has advanced with the progress of their other enjoyments. The linsey-woolsey garments which formerly served as a harbour for dirt, both to males and females, have been thrown aside, and their place occupied by others more flexible and oftener renewed. This may be the cause in part of the immense increase in the quantity of soap for which the duty is paid. Within the last forty years it has gradually increased from thirty-five to ninety-five million pounds. . . .

DOCUMENT 150

William Cobbett, Rural Rides, Vol II, p 348

Go down into the villages . . . and then look at the miserable sheds in which the labourers reside! Look at these hovels, made of mud and straw, bits of glass, or old cast-off windows, without frames or hinges frequently but merely stuck in the mud-wall. Enter them and look at the bits of chairs or stools; the wretched boards tacked together to serve for a table; the floor of pebble, broken brick or of the bare ground; look at the thing called a bed; and survey the rags on the backs of the wretched inhabitants.

A Country Diet

DOCUMENT 151

The Family Oracle of Health (1827), Vol V
Quoted in J. C. Drummond and A. Wilbraham, The Englishman's Food

The diet of persons who live in the country is, in general, more wholesome than that of those who inhabit towns. A large portion of it consists of fresh vegetables and milk, which, though not excluded from the food of those who live in towns, are enjoyed in much greater plenty and higher perfection in rural situations.

The End of Living-In

DOCUMENT 152

Lords Committee on the Poor Law, Parliamentary Papers VIII, 1830–1,
pp 26–7
Quoted in E. J. Hobsbawm and George Rude, Captain Swing

When I was a boy I used to visit a large Farmhouse, where the Farmer sat in a room with a Door opening to the Servants' Hall and everything was carried from one Table to the other. Now they will rarely permit a Man to live in their Houses; and it is in consequence a total Bargain and Sale for Money, and all Idea of Affection is destroyed.

The Labourers' Revolt

The Greville Memoirs, 21st November 1830

In the meantime the new Government will find plenty to occupy their most serious thoughts and employ their best talents. The state of the country is dreadful; every post brings fresh accounts of conflagrations, destruction of machinery, association of labourers, and compulsory rise of wages. Cobbett and Carlisle write and harangue to inflame the minds of the people, who are already set in motion and excited by all the events which have happened abroad. Distress is certainly not the cause of these commotions, for the people have patiently supported far greater privations than they had been exposed to before these riots, and the country was generally in an improving state.

The Duke of Richmond went down to Sussex and had a battle with a mob of 200 labourers, whom he beat with fifty of his own farmers and tenants, harangued them, and sent them away in good humour. He is, however, very popular. In Hants the disturbances have been dreadful. There was an assemblage of 1,000 or 1,500 men, part of whom went towards Baring's house (the Grange) after destroying threshing-machines and other agricultural implements; they were met by Bingham Baring, who attempted to address them, when a fellow (who had been employed at a guinea a week by his father up to four days before) knocked him down with an iron bar and nearly killed him. They have no troops in that part of the country, and there is a depot of arms at Winchester.

The Condition of the Labourer

Quote from Liberal Member of Parliament 1830
E. G. Wakefield, Swing Unmasked; or, The Cause of Rural Incendiarism
(1831)

An English agricultural labourer and an English pauper, these words are synonymous. His father was a pauper and his mother's milk contained no nourishment. From his earliest childhood he had bad food, and only half enough to still his hunger, and even yet he undergoes the pangs of unsatisfied hunger almost all the time that he is not asleep. He is half clad, and has not more fire than barely suffices to cook his scanty meal. And so cold and damp are always at home with him, and leave him only in fine weather. He is married, but he knows nothing of the joys of the husband and father. His wife and children, hungry, rarely warm, often ill and helpless, always careworn and hopeless like himself, are naturally grasping, selfish, and trouble-some, and so, to use his own expression, he hates the sight of them, and enters his cot only because it offers him a trifle more shelter from rain and wind than a hedge. He must support his family, though he cannot do so, whence come beggary, deceit of all sorts, ending in fully developed craftiness. If he were so inclined, he yet has not the courage which makes of the more energetic of his class wholesale poachers and smugglers. But he pilfers when occasion offers, and teaches his children to lie and steal. His abject and sub-missive demeanour towards his wealthy neighbours shows that they treat him roughly and with suspicion; hence he fears and hates them, but he never will injure them by force. He is depraved through and through, too far gone to possess even the strength of despair. His wretched existence is brief, rheumatism and asthma bring him to the workhouse, where he will draw his last breath without a single pleasant recollection, and will make room for another luckless wretch to live and die as he has done.

The Rural Revolution

DOCUMENT 155

K. Marx, Das Kapital (1867), Vol I, p 554

In the sphere of agriculture, modern industry has a more revolutionary effect than elsewhere, for this reason, that it annihilates the peasant, that bulwark of the old society, and replaces him by the wage labourer. Thus the desire for social changes, and the class antagonisms are brought to the same level in the country as in the towns.

The Effects of Drudgery

DOCUMENT 156

Charles Kingsley, Yeast (1848)

At dusk the same evening the two (Lancelot and Tregarva) had started for the village fair. As they walked together along the plashy turnpike road, overtaking, now and then, groups of two or three who were out on the same errand as themselves, Lancelot could not help remarking to the keeper how superior was the look of comfort in the boys and young men, with their ruddy cheeks and smart dress, to the worn and haggard appearance of the elder men.

'Let them alone, poor fellows,' said Tregarva; 'it won't last long. When they've got two or three children at their heels, they'll look as thin and shabby as their own fathers.'

'They must spend a great deal of money on their clothes.'

'And on their stomachs, too, sir. They never lay by a farthing; and I don't see how they can, when their club-money's paid, and their insides are well filled.'

'Do you mean to say that they actually have not as much to eat after they marry?'

'Indeed and I do, sir. They get no more wages afterwards round here and have four or five to clothe and feed off the same money that used to keep one; and that sum won't take long to work out, I think?'

'But do they not, in some places, pay the married men higher wages than the unmarried?'

'That's a worse trick still, sir; for it tempts the poor thoughtless boys to go and marry the first girl they can get hold of; and it don't want much persuasion to make them do that at any time.'

'But why don't the clergymen teach them to put into the savings' banks?'

'One here and there, sir, says what he can: though it's of very little use. Besides, every one is afraid of savings' banks now; not a year but one reads of some breaking, and the lawyers going off with the earnings of the poor. And if they didn't, youth's a foolish time at best; and the carnal man will be hankering after amusement, sir—amusement.'

'And no wonder,' said Lancelot; 'at all events, I should not think they got much out of it. But it does seem strange that no higher amusement can be found for them than the beer-shop. Can't they read? Can't they practise light and interesting handicrafts at home, as the German peasantry do?'

'Who'll teach 'em, sir? From the plough-tail to the reaping hook, and back again, is all they know. Besides, sir, they are not like us, Cornish; they are a stupid pig-headed generation at the best, these south countrymen. They're grown-up babies, who want the parson and the squire to be leading them, and preaching to them, and spurring them on, and coaxing them up every moment. And as for scholarship, sir, a boy leaves school at nine or ten to follow the horses; and between that time and his wedding-day he forgets every word he learnt, and becomes for the most part as thorough a heathen savage at heart as those wild Indians in the Brazil's used to be.'

'And then we call them civilised English-men!' said Lancelot. 'We can see that your Indian is a savage, because he wears skins and feathers; but your Irish cotter or your English Labourer, because he happens to wear a coat and trousers, is considered to be a civilised man.'

'It's the way of the world, sir,' said Tregarva, 'judging carnal judgment, according to the sight of its own eyes; always looking at the outside of things and men, sir, and never much deeper. But as for the reading, sir, it's all very well for me, who have been a keeper and dawdled about like a gentleman with a gun over my arm; but did you ever do a good day's farm-work in your life? If you had, man or boy, you wouldn't have been game for much reading when you got home; you'd do just what these poor fellows do—tumble into bed at eight o'clock, hardly waiting to take your clothes off, knowing that you must turn up again at five o'clock the next morning to get a breakfast of bread, and perhaps, a dab of the squire's dripping, and then back to work again; and so on, day after day, sir, week after week, year after year, without a hope or a chance of being anything but what you are, and only too thankful if you can get work to break your back, and catch the rheumatism over.'

'But do you mean to say that their labour is so severe and incessant?'

'It's only God's blessing if it is incessant, sir; for if it stops, they starve, or go to the house to be worse fed than the thieves in gaol. And as for its being severe, there's many a boy, as their mothers will tell you, comes home, night after night, too tired to eat their suppers, and tumble, fasting, to bed in the same foul shirt which they've been working in all day, never changing their rag of calico from week's end to week's end, or washing the sink that's under it once in seven years.'

'No wonder,' said Lancelot, 'that such a life of drudgery makes them brutal and reckless.'

'No wonder, indeed, sir; they've no time to think; they're born to be machines, and machines they must be; and I think, sir,' he added bitterly, 'it's God's mercy that they daren't think. It's God's mercy that they don't feel. Men that write books and talk at elections call this a free country, and say that the poorest and meanest has a free opening to rise and become prime minister if he can. But you see, sir, the misfortune is, that in practice he can't; for one who gets into a gentleman's family, or into a little shop, and so saves a few pounds, fifty know that they've no chance before them, but day-labourer born, day-labourer live, from hand to mouth, scraping and pinching to get not meat and beer even, but bread and potatoes; and then, at the end of it all, for a worthy reward, half-acrown a week of parish-pay—or the workhouse. That's lively, hopeful prospect for a Christian man!'

'But,' said Lancelot, 'I thought this New Poor Law was to stir them up to independence?'

'Oh, sir, the old law has bit too deep: it made them slaves and beggars at heart. It taught them not to be ashamed of parish pay—to demand it as a right.'

'And so it is their right,' said Lancelot. 'In God's name, if a country is so ill-constituted that it cannot find its own citizens in work, it is bound to find them in food.'

'May be, sir, maybe. God knows I don't grudge it them. It's a poor pittance at best, when they have got it. But don't you see, sir, how all poor-laws, old or new either, sucks the independent spirit out of a man; how they make the poor wretches reckless; how they tempt him to spend every farthing extra in amusement?'

'How, then?'

'Why, he is always tempted to say to himself, "Whatever happens to me, the parish must keep me. If I am sick, it must doctor me; if I am worn out, it must feed me: if I die it must bury me; if I leave my children paupers, the parish must look after them, and they'll be as well off with the parish as they were with me. Now they've only got just enough to keep body and soul together, and the parish can't give them less than that. What's the use of cutting myself off from sixpenny-worth of pleasure here, and sixpenny-worth there. I'm not saving money for my children, I'm only saving the farmer's rates." There it is, sir,' said Tregarva; 'that's the bottom of it, sir—"I'm only saving the farmer's rates." "Let us eat and drink for tomorrow we die!"'

Effect of the Railways

DOCUMENT 157

R. D. Baxter, Railway Extension and its Results (1866)
Quoted in Essays in Econonic History, Vol 3, ed. Canis-Wilson

Free Trade benefited the manufacturing populations, but had little to do with the agriculturalists. Yet the distress in the rural districts was as great or greater than in the towns, and this under a system of the most rigid Protection. How did the country population attain their present prosperity? Simply by the emigration to the towns or colonies of the redundant labourers. This emigration was scarcely possible till the construction of the railways. Up to that time the farm labourer was unable to migrate; from that time he became a migratory animal. The increase of population in agricultural counties stopped, or was changed into a decrease, and the labourers ceased to be too numerous for the work. To this cause is principally owing the sufficiency of employment and wages throughout the agricultural portion of the kingdom. If I may venture on a comparison, England was, in 1830, like a wide-spreading plain, flooded with stagnant waters, which were the cause of malaria and distress. Railways were a grand system of drainage, carrying away to the running streams, or to the ocean, the redundant moisture, and restoring the country to fertility and prosperity.

Industrial Society

Preface

Mid-Victorian Britain was the 'workshop of the world' and the cynosure of social observation. Britain was to the nineteenth century what America is to the twentieth—an image of the future, with all its attendant wonders and new social problems. 'The Condition of England question' was debated primarily *in* England, though the discussion was informed by the observations of European and American visitors, to whom the historian is indebted for their general speculation on the nature of English society. English writers, true to their empirical tradition, and conditioned by the fact that they were themselves participants in the process they sought to analyse, tended to focus attention on specific aspects of the emergent industrial Britain in which there were as many townsmen as countrymen by 1851.

The Rise of the Bourgeoisie

DOCUMENT 158

Karl Marx and Friedrich Engels, The Communist Manifesto, pp 45-55

Our epoch, the epoch of the bourgeoisie, possesses . . . this distinctive feature; it has simplified the class antagonisms. Society as a whole is more and more splitting up into two great hostile camps, into two great classes directly facing each other: Bourgeoisie and Proletariat.

.   .   .   .   .

Modern industry has established the world market, for which the discovery of America paved the way. This market has given an immense development to commerce, to navigation, to communication by land. This development has, in its turn, reacted on the extension of industry; and in proportion as industry, commerce, navigation, railways extended, in the same proportion the bourgeoisie developed, increased its capital, and pushed into the background every class handed down from the Middle Ages.

We see, therefore, how the modern bourgeoisie is itself the product of a long course of development, of a series of revolutions in the modes of production and of exchange.

Each step in the development of the bourgeoisie was accompanied by a corresponding political advance of that class.

. . . . . .

The bourgeoisie, wherever it has got the upper hand, has put an end to all feudal, patriarchal, idyllic relations. It has pitilessly torn asunder the motley feudal ties that bound man to his 'natural superiors' and has left remaining no other nexus between man and man but naked self-interest, than callous 'cash-payment'. It has drowned the most heavenly ecstasies of religious fervour, of chivalrous enthusiasm, of philistine sentimentalism, in the icy water of egotistical calculation. It has resolved personal worth into exchange value, and in place of the numberless indefeasible chartered freedoms, has set up that single, unconscionable freedom—Free Trade. In one word, for exploitation, veiled by religious and political illusions, it has substituted naked, shameless, direct, brutal exploitation.

. . . . . .

The bourgeoisie, by the rapid improvement of all instruments of production, by the immensely facilitated means of communication, draws all, even the most barbarian, nations into civilisation. The cheap prices of its commodities are the heavy artillery with which it batters down all Chinese walls, with which it forces the barbarians' intensely obstinate hatred of foreigners to capitulate. It compels all nations, upon pain of extinction, to adopt the bourgeois mode of production; it compels them to introduce what it calls civilisation into their midst i.e. to become bourgeois themselves. In one word, it creates a world after its own image.

. . . . . .

In proportion as the bourgeoisie i.e. capital, is developed, in the same proportion is the proletariat, the modern working class developed. . . . These labourers, who must sell themselves piecemeal, are a commodity, like every other article of commerce, and are consequently exposed to all the vicissitudes of competition, to all the fluctuations of the market.

Owing to the extensive use of machinery and to division of labour, the work of the proletarians has lost all individual character, and, consequently, all charm for the workman. He becomes an appendage of the machine, and it is only the most simple, most monotonous, and most easily acquired knack, that is required of him. . . . Masses of labourers, crowded into the factory, are organised like soldiers. As privates of the industrial army they are placed under the command of a perfect hierarchy of officers and sergeants. Not only are they slaves of the bourgeois class, and of the bourgeois state;

they are daily and hourly enslaved by the machine, by the over-looker, and, above all, by the individual bourgeois manufacturer himself. . . .

The less the skill and exertion of strength implied in manual labour, in other words, the more modern industry becomes developed, the more is the labour of men superseded by that of women. Differences of age and sex have no longer any distinctive social validity for the working class. All are instruments of labour, more or less expensive to use, according to their age and sex.

Cotton-Masters and Cotton Spinners

DOCUMENT 159

Black Dwarf, 30th September 1818
Quoted in E. P. Thompson, The Making of the English Working Class

First, then, as to the employers: with very few exceptions, they are a set of men who have sprung from the cotton-shop without education or address, except so much as they have acquired by their intercourse with the little world of merchants on the exchange at Manchester; but to counterbalance that deficiency, they give you enough of appearances by an ostentatious display of elegant mansions, equipages, liveries, parks, hunters, hounds, etc. which they take care to shew off to the merchant stranger in the most pompous manner. Indeed their houses are gorgeous palaces, far surpassing in bulk and extent the neat charming retreats you see round London . . . but the chaste observer of the beauties of nature and art combined will observe a woeful deficiency of taste. They bring up their families at the most costly schools, determined to give their offspring a double portion of what they were so deficient in themselves. Thus with scarcely a second idea in their heads, they are literally petty monarchs, absolute and despotic, in their own particular districts; and to support all this, their whole time is occupied in contriving how to get the greatest quantity of work turned off with the least expence. . . . In short, I will venture to say, without fear of contradiction, that there is a greater distance observed between the master there and the spinner, than there is between the first merchant in London and his lowest servant or the lowest artisan. Indeed there is no comparison. I know it to be a fact, that the greater part of the master spinners are anxious to keep wages low for the purpose of keeping the spinners indigent and spiritless . . . as for the purpose of taking the surplus to their own pockets.

The master spinners are a class of men unlike all other master tradesmen in the kingdom. They are ignorant, proud, and tyrannical. What then must be the men or rather beings who are the instruments of such masters? Why, they have been for a series of years, with their wives and their families, patience itself—bondmen and bondwomen to their cruel taskmasters. It is in vain to insult our common understandings with the observation that such men are free; that the law protects the rich and poor alike, and that a spinner can leave his master if he does not like the wages. True; so he can: but where must he go? why to another, to be sure. Well: he goes; he is asked where did you work last: 'did he discharge you?' No; we could not agree about wages. Well I shall not employ you nor anyone who leaves his master in that manner. Why is this? Because there is an abominable combination existing amongst the masters, first established at Stockport in 1802, and it has since become so general, as to embrace all the great masters for a circuit of many miles round Manchester, though not the little masters: they are excluded. They are the most obnoxious beings to the great ones that can be imagined ... When the combination first took place, one of their first articles was, that no master should take on a man until he had first ascertained whether his last master had discharged him. What then is the man to do? If he goes to the parish, that grave of all independence, he is there told— We shall not relieve you; if you dispute with your master, and don't support your family, we will send you to prison; so that the man is bound, by a combination of circumstances, to submit to his master. He cannot travel and get work in any town like a shoe-maker, joiner, or taylor; he is confined to the district.

The workmen in general are an inoffensive, unassuming set of well-informed men, though how they acquire their information is almost a mystery to me. They are docile and tractable, if not goaded too much; but this is not to be wondered at, when we consider that they are trained to work from six years old, from five in a morning to eight and nine at night. Let one of the advocates for obedience to his master take his stand in an avenue leading to a factory a little before five o'clock in the morning, and observe the squalid appearance of the little infants and their parents taken from their beds at so early an hour in all kinds of weather; let him examine the miserable pittance of food, chiefly composed of water gruel and oatcake broken into it, a little salt, and sometimes coloured with a little milk, together with a few potatoes, and a bit of bacon or fat for dinner; would a London mechanic eat this? There they are (and if late a few minutes, a quarter of a day is stopped in wages) locked up until night in rooms heated above the hottest days we have had this summer, and allowed no time, except three-quarters of an hour at dinner in the whole day: whatever they eat at any other time must be as they are at work. The negro slave in the West Indies, if he works under a scorching sun, has probably a little breeze of air sometimes to fan him: he has a space of ground, and time allowed to cultivate it. The English spinner slave has no enjoyment of the open atmosphere and breezes of heaven. Locked up in factories eight stories high, he has no relaxation till the ponderous engine stops, and then he goes home to get refreshed for the next day; no time for sweet association with his family; they are all alike fatigued and exhausted. This is no over-drawn picture; it is literally true; I ask again, would the mechanics in the South of England submit to this?

When the spinning of cotton was in its infancy, and before those terrible machines for superseding the necessity of human labour, called steam engines, came into use, there were a great number of what were then called little masters; men who with a small capital, could procure a few machines, and employ a few hands, men and boys (say to twenty or thirty), the produce of whose labour was all taken to Manchester central mart, and put into the hands of brokers. . . . The brokers sold it to the merchants, by which means the master spinner was enabled to stay at home and work and attend to his workmen. The cotton was then always given out in its raw state from the bale to the wives of the spinners at home, when they heat and cleansed it ready for the spinners in the factory. By this they could earn eight, ten, or twelve shillings a week, and cook and attend to their families. But none are thus employed now; for all the cotton is broke up by a machine, turned by the steam engine, called a devil: so that the spinners' wives have no employment, except they go to work in the factory all day at what can be done by children for a few shillings, four or five per week. If a man then could not agree with his master, he left him, and could get employed elsewhere. A few years, however, changed the face of things. Steam engines came into use, to purchase which, and to erect buildings sufficient to contain them and six or seven hundred hands, required a great capital. The engine power produced a more marketable (though not a better) article than the little master could at the same price. The consequence was their ruin in a short time; and the overgrown capitalists triumphed in their fall; for they were the only obstacle that stood between them and the complete control of the workmen.

Various disputes then originated between the workmen and masters as to the fineness of the work, the workmen being paid according to the numbers of hanks or yards of thread he produced from a given quantity of cotton, which was always to be proved by the overlooker, whose interest made it imperative on him to lean to his master, and call the material coarser than it was. If the workman would not submit he must summon his employer before a magistrate; the whole of the acting magistrates in that district, with the exception of the two worthy clergymen, being gentlemen who have sprung from the same source with the master cotton spinners. The employer generally contented himself with sending his overlooker to answer any such summons, thinking it beneath him to meet his servant. The magistrate's decision was generally in favour of the master, though on the statement of the overlooker only. The workman dared not appeal to the sessions on account of the expense. . . .

These evils to the men have arisen from that dreadful monopoly which exists in those districts where wealth and power are got into the hands of the few, who, in the pride of their hearts, think themselves the lords of the universe.

DOCUMENT 160

W. Thompson, Tour of England and Scotland (1788), p 11
Quoted in Asa Briggs, How They Lived, 1700–1815

May 19th. Leave Stratford. . . . In the evening arrive at Birmingham; but this being unfortunately the time of their fair, we could not see any of the manufacturers at work. Visit Clay's manufactory for making tea-boards, buttons, and other articles pasted together and dried. Visit also Boulton's manufactory for plated articles of all sorts of steel and iron-work. This town is very extensive, and a great part of it elegantly built. It contains upwards of one hundred thousand inhabitants; but the people are all diminutive in size, and sickly in their appearance, from their sedentary employment. In Birmingham there is one very elegant and spacious church, three chapels, and eight meeting-houses for Dissenters . . . but the great mass of the people give themselves very little concern about religious matters, seldom, if ever, going to church, and spending the Sundays in their ordinary working apparel, in low debauchery. What religion there is in Birmingham is to be found among the Dissenters. It is well known that there are many coiners of false money in Birmingham, a circumstance that is easily accounted for, from the nature of the business in which they have been accustomed to be employed. It may be added, that there is a great deal of trick and low cunning among the Birmingham manufacturers in general, though there are, no doubt, some exceptions, as well as profligacy of manners. This may be owing in part, to their want of early education; for the moment that the children are fit for any kind of labour, instead of being sent to school, they are set to some sort of work or other: but it is probably more owing to their being constantly associated together both in their labouring and in their idle hours. It is remarkable, that society corrupts the manners of the vulgar as much as it sharpens their understanding.

About fifty years ago, there were only three principal or leading streets in Birmingham, which at this day is so crowded, and at the same time so extensive a town: a circumstance which illustrates, in a very striking manner, the rapid increase of our manufactures and trade in steel and iron.

The manufacturers of Birmingham who are generally accounted rich, are such as possess fortunes from five to fifteen thousand pounds. A few are in possession of much larger capitals; but in general, they may be said to be in easy and flourishing circumstances, rather than very rich or affluent. The number of carriages kept by private persons has been doubled within these ten years: so also has that of the women of the town. These different species of luxury seem to have advanced in proportions pretty nearly equal. The people of Birmingham have often tried to establish a coffee-house; but found this impossible, even with the advantage of a subscription. they generally resort to ale-houses and taverns. According to the size of the place, there should be several coffee-houses, taking our standard in this matter, from London. But the genius of Birmingham is not that of coffee-houses.

A Manufacturer's City

DOCUMENT 161 ✗

Manchester (2nd July 1835)
De Tocqueville—Journey to England

PECULIAR CHARACTER OF MANCHESTER

The great manufacturing city for cloth, thread, cotton . . . as is Birmingham for iron, copper, steel.

Favourable circumstances: ten leagues from the largest port in England, which is the best-placed port in Europe for receiving raw materials from America safely and quickly. Close by the largest coal-mines to keep the machines going cheaply. Twenty-five leagues away, the place where the best machines in the world are made. Three canals and a railway quickly carry the products all over England, and over the whole world.

The employers are helped by science, industry, the love of gain and English capital. Among the workers are men coming from a country where the needs of men are reduced almost to those of savages, and who can work for a very low wage, and so keep down the level of wages for the English workmen who wish to compete, to almost the same level. So there is the combination of the advantages of a rich and of a poor country; of an ignorant and an enlightened people; of civilisation and barbarism.

So it is not surprising that Manchester already has 300,000 inhabitants and is growing at a prodigious rate.

OTHER DIFFERENCES BETWEEN MANCHESTER AND BIRMINGHAM

The police are less efficient at Manchester than at Birmingham. More complete absence of government; 60,000 Irish at Manchester (at most 5,000 at Birmingham); a crowd of small tenants huddled in the same house. At Birmingham almost all the houses are inhabited by one family only; at Manchester a part of the population lives in damp cellars, hot, stinking and unhealthy; thirteen to fifteen individuals in one. At Birmingham that is rare. At Manchester, stagnant puddles, roads paved badly or not at all. Insufficient public lavatories. All that almost unknown at Birmingham. At Manchester a few great capitalists, thousands of poor workmen and little middle class. At Birmingham, few large industries, many small industrialists. At Manchester workmen are counted by the thousand, two or three thousand in the factories. At Birmingham the workers work in their own houses or in little workshops in company with the master himself. At Manchester there is above all need for women and children. At Birmingham, particularly men, few women. From the look of the inhabitants of Manchester, the working people of Birmingham seem more healthy, better off, more orderly and more moral than those of Manchester.

DOCUMENT 162

F. Engels, Condition of the Working Class in England
Quoted in E. J. Hobsbawm, The Age of Revolution: 1798–1848, p 218

One day I walked with one of these middle-class gentlemen into Manchester. I spoke to him about the disgraceful unhealthy slums and drew his attention to the disgusting condition of that part of town in which the factory workers lived. I declared that I had never seen so badly built a town in my life. He listened patiently and at the corner of the street at which we parted company, he remarked: 'And yet there is a great deal of money made here. Good morning, Sir!'

DOCUMENT 163

Canon Parkinson 'On the Present Condition of the Labouring Poor in Manchester' (1841)
Quoted in Asa Briggs, Victorian Cities, p 114

There is no town in the world where the distance between the rich and the poor is so great, or the barrier between them so difficult to be crossed. I once ventured to designate the town of Manchester the most *aristocratic* town in England; and, in the sense in which the term was used, the expression is not hyperbolical. The separation between the different classes, and the consequent ignorance of each other's habits and condition, are far more complete in this place than in any country of the older nations of Europe, or the agricultural parts of our own kingdom. There is far less *personal* communication between the master cotton spinner and his workmen, between the calico printer and his blue-handed boys, between the master tailor and his apprentices, than there is between the Duke of Wellington and the humblest labourer on his estate, or than there *was* between good old George the Third and the meanest errand-boy about his palace. I mention this not as a matter of blame, but I state it simply as a *fact*.

Land and Social Esteem

DOCUMENT 164

De Tocqueville—Journey to England
Sharp, Lawyer and Radical (8th May 1835)

Q. What do the common people in England do with their money when they have any to spare?

A. They spend it in orgies or they put it into business.

Q. Have they the idea of buying land?

A. Not at all. Such an idea would never enter the head of an English peasant.

Q. Why is that?

A. Partly because the English countryman never sees small landed properties, and also because commerce offers many more openings here than in France.

Q. Thus everyone who rises above the working classes goes into commerce or industry?

A. Yes.

Q. Thus when the poor man sees before him a landowner who himself alone possesses half a county, the idea does not strike him that this immense property divided between all the inhabitants of the neighbourhood, could give comfort to each of them, and he does not regard this great landowner as a sort of common enemy?

A. No. That feeling has not yet been born. I repeat that the taste for real estate is a taste of the rich man. When one becomes a millionaire by trade, one buys a large estate which brings in hardly 2 per cent, and which entails much showy expenditure, but at the same time gives you a high social position

The English Aristocracy

DOCUMENT 165

A. de Tocqueville, Journey to England (1835)

In England an illustrious name is a great advantage and a cause of much pride to him who bears it, but in general one can say that the aristocracy is founded on wealth, a thing which may be *acquired*, and not on birth which cannot. From this it results that one can clearly see in England where the aristocracy begins, but it is impossible to say where it ends. It could be compared to the Rhine whose source is to be found on the peak of a high mountain, but which divides into a thousand little streams and, in a manner of speaking, disappears before it reaches the sea. The difference between England and France in this matter turns on the examination of a single word in each language. 'Gentleman' and 'gentilhomme' evidently have the same derivation, but 'gentleman' in England is applied to every well-educated man whatever his birth, while in France *gentilhomme* applies only to a noble by birth. The meaning of these two words of common origin has been so transformed by the different social climates of the two countries that today they simply cannot be translated, at least without recourse to a periphrasis. This grammatical observation is more illuminating than many long arguments.

The English aristocracy can therefore never arouse those violent hatreds felt by the middle and lower classes against the nobility in France where the nobility is an exclusive caste, which while monopolising all privileges and hurting everybody's feelings, offers no hope of ever entering into its ranks.

The English aristocracy has a hand in everything; it is open to everyone; and anyone who wishes to abolish it or attack it as a body, would have a hard task to define the object of his onslaught.

DOCUMENT 166

Speech by Richard Cobden, 1845
Quoted in D. G. Barnes, History of the Corn Laws, pp 265–6

You gentlemen of England, the high aristocracy of England, your forefathers led my forefathers; you may lead us again if you choose; but though—longer than any other aristocracy—you have kept your power, while the battle-fields and the hunting-field were the tests of manly vigour, you have not done as the noblesse of France or the hidalgos of Madrid have done: you have been Englishmen, not wanting in courage on any call. But this is a new age; the age of social advancement, not of feudal sports; you belong to a mercantile age; you cannot have the advantage of commercial rents and retain your feudal privileges, too. If you identify yourselves with the spirit of the age, you may yet do well; for I tell you that the people of this country look to their aristocracy with a deep-rooted prejudice—an hereditary prejudice, I may call it—in their favour; but your power was never got, and you will not keep it by obstructing that progressive spirit of the age in which you live. If you are found obstructing that progressive spirit which is calculated to knit nations more closely together by commercial intercourse; if you give nothing but opposition to schemes which almost give life and breath to inanimate nature, and which it has been decreed shall go on, then you are not longer a national body.

DOCUMENT 167

Speeches of John Bright (1868), Vol 2, pp 275–6
19th December 1845, at Covent Garden

. . . I believe this to be a movement of the commercial and industrious classes against the lords and great proprietors of the soil. . . .

We have had landlord rule longer, far longer than the life of the oldest man in this vast assembly, and I would ask you to look at the results of that rule. . . . The landowners have had unlimited sway in Parliament and in the provinces. Abroad, the history of our country is the history of war and rapine: at home, of debt, taxes, and rapine too. . . . We find them legislating corruptly: they pray daily that in their legislation they may discard all private ends and partial affections, and after prayers they sit down to make a law for the purpose of extorting from all the consumers of food a higher price than it is worth, that the extra price may find its way into the pockets of the proprietors of land, these proprietors being the very men by whom this infamous law is sustained. . . .

The Poor Man Pays for All

DOCUMENT 168

A New Hunting Song (c. 1846)
Quoted in The Common Muse

Now those that are low spirited I hope won't think it wrong,
While I sing to you a verse or two of a new hunting song;
For the hunting season has set in, or else just now begun,
Our heroes all will have their fun with the dog and gun.

Chorus
And a hunting they will go, will go,
And a hunting they will go, will go!
They'll use all means, and try all schemes,
For to keep the poor man low.

With one of our brave huntsmen, I'm going to commence,
His name it was bold Bonaparte, he was a man of sense;
He hunted off from Corsica upon a game of Chance,
And hunted until he became the Emperor of France.

The next huntsman was Wellington, he'd the best of luck,
He hunted from Lieutenant, till he became a Duke,
His men did fight well for him, and did his honour gain,
He done his best endeavours to have their pensions taken.

As for our hero Nelson, he hunted well for fame,
He was as bold a huntsman as e'er hunted on the main:
And for his warlike valour, he always bore the sway,
Till a cannon ball caused his downfall, all in Trafalgar Bay.

Prince Albert to this country came hunting for a wife,
He got one whom he loved dear as his own life;
Oh yes, a blooming little Queen for to dandle on his knee
With thirty thousand pounds a year paid from this country.

O'Connell he went hunting all through old Ireland's vale,
And says he'll go on hunting until he gets repeal.
They swear they'll have a Parliament in Dublin once more,
And make the trade to flourish all round green Erin's shore.

John Frost in Wales a hunting went, and well knew how to ride,
He had a fine bred Chartist horse, but got on the wrong side,
If he had held the reins quite firm in his own hand,
They'd ne'er have hunted him into Van Diemans Land.

The Queen she went a hunting thro' Scotland and France,
She hunted foreign countries through to learn the Polka dance;
Bobby Peel, he's a huntsman bold, was never known to fail,
He hunted up the Income Tax, and then the Corn Law Bill.

They're hunting up the poor man, he's hunted every day,
And hawkers too, if they do not a heavy licence pay.
They won't allow the poor to beg, it is a crime to steal,
For the one there's the Union, for the other there's the gaol.

So to conclude my hunting song, I hope you'll all agree
While the poor are starved and hunted down, the rich will have their spree.
To complain is quite a crime, for poor you're to remain,
The Parson says, if you're content, Heaven you're sure to gain.

The Problem of Poverty

The Decline of Traditional Charity

By the middle of the eighteenth century the competitive, rationalist spirit seems to have been eroding traditional charity and the social responsibility practised by earlier generations towards the more vulnerable members of society.

DOCUMENT 169

All Things be Dear but Poor Men's Labour or The Sad Complaint of Poor People
Quoted in the Common Muse, edited by V. de Sola Pinto

Being a true Relation to the dearness of all kind of Food, to the great Grief and Sorrow of many Thousands in this Nation. Likewise, the uncharitableness of Rich Men to the Poor. This Song was begun at Worcester, the middle at Shrewsbury, the end at Coventry by L.W.

> Kind Country-men listen I pray
>   unto this my harmless Ditty,
> Observe these words which I shall say
>   for it is true the mores the pitty;
> But chief to those that stand me by,
>   whether stranger or my neighbour
> I think there's none than can deny
>   all things are dear but poorman's labour
>
> We find that Bread-Corn now is dear,
>   in every Town throughout this Nation,
> The Rich now poor men will not bear
>   because Charity's out of fashion,
> Poor men do work all day and night
>   for that which in it hath small favour,
> A Loaf of sixpence is but small
>   all things are dear but poorman's labour
>
> Beef and Mutton is so dear
>   a mans weeks wages cannot buy it,
>   all things are dear who can deny it,

But poor mens labour is too cheap
    and Tra(d)ing's dead which makes times harder
That all their pains wont find them meat
    all things are dear but poorman's labour

Is it not sad for Parents now
    to hear their children for bread crying,
And has it not for them to give
    although for food they lye a dying,
Poor little Babies they must fast
    although it grieves Mother and Father,
A bit of bread they cannot tast,
    all things are dear but poorman's labour

To hear the many sad Complaints
    as I have heard in Town and City,
I think you'd cry as well as I,
    the Rich has for the Poor no pitty
For if they work now for Rich men
    there some, will keep their Wages from them
And make them run to and agan,
    Which makes the poor cry fye upon them.
    all things are dear but poorman's labour

Farmers so covetous they be
    Their Corn they'l hoard for better profit
Although the Poor do fast we see,
    their grain they'l keep what ere comes of it.
Whole Ricks of Corn stands in their yards
    and scorns to show the Poor some favour
For some do swear they do not care
    if things be dear, but poor mans labour

A Rich man there was in Staffordshire,
    which is a knave, I'm sure no better
He hoped to sell his Corn so dear (as others) do
    their Pepper,
When Wheat was sold for shillings ten
    he would not Thrash, Fan, nor yet rake it
Let poor despair he oft did swear
    heed keep it for a better market

The Social Value of Poverty

To many observers poverty was a necessary ingredient in the social order, rather than an obvious evil to be eliminated.

DOCUMENT 170

J. Townsend, A Dissertation on the Poor Laws (1786)
Quoted in Asa Briggs

It seems to be a law of nature, that the poor should be to a certain degree improvident, that there may always be some to fulfil the most servile, the most sordid, and the most ignoble offices in the community. The stock of human happiness is thereby much increased, whilst the more delicate are not only relieved from drudgery, and freed from those occasional employments which would make them miserable, but are left at liberty, without interruption, to pursue those callings which are suited to their various dispositions, and most useful to the State. As for the lowest of the poor, by custom they are reconciled to the meanest occupations, to the most laborious works, and to the most hazardous pursuits; whilst the hope of their reward makes them cheerful in the midst of all their dangers and their toils. The fleets and armies of a state would soon be in want of soldiers and of sailors if sobriety and diligence universally prevailed: for what is it but distress and poverty which can prevail upon the lower classes of people to encounter all the horrors which await them on the tempestuous ocean, or in the field of battle? Men who are easy in their circumstances are not among the foremost to engage in a seafaring or military life. There must be a degree of pressure, and that which is attended with the least violence will be the best. When hunger is either felt or feared, the desire of obtaining bread will quietly dispose the mind to undergo the greatest hardships, and will sweeten the severest labours.

The Poorhouse

For the casualties of society the poorhouse represented the last resort before starvation. Many were well run, others did their best to exploit the unwilling labour of their inmates. Conditions seem to have varied greatly from one area to another.

DOCUMENT 171

Crabbe, The Village, Book I

> There, in yon house, that holds the parish poor,
> Whose walls of mud scarce bear the broken door;

There, where the putrid vapours, flagging, play,
And the dull wheel hums doleful through the day—
There children dwell, who know no parents' care;
Parents, who know no children's love, dwell there!
Heartbroken matrons on their joyless bed,
Forsaken wives, and mothers never wed;
Dejected widows with unheeded tears;
And crippled age with more than childhood fears;
The lame, the blind, and, far the happiest they!
The moping idiot, and the madman gay.
Here too the sick their final doom receive,
Here brought, amid the scenes of grief, to grieve,
Where the loud groans from some sad chamber flow,
Mix'd with the clamour of the crowd below,
Here, sorrowing, they each kindred sorrow scan,
And the cold charities of man to man.

Poverty—the moral failure

Fluctuations in earnings encouraged the labouring poor to spend wastefully in periods of prosperity and fall into debt in periods of unemployment. The level of total income received was important, but so was the regularity with which it was earned.

DOCUMENT 172

Sir F. M. Eden, The State of the Poor (1797), Book II, Ch. II, p 495

There seems to be just reason to conclude that the miseries of the labouring Poor arose, less from the scantiness of their income (however much the philanthropist might wish it to be increased) than from their own improvidence and unthriftiness; since it is the fact, and I trust will be demonstrated in a subsequent part of this work, that in many parts of the kingdom, where the earnings of industry are moderate, the condition of the labourers is more comfortable than in other districts where wages are exorbitant. . . .

The Old Poor Law in Action

Throughout the war years, when the population was rising rapidly, when prices were high and social discontent always threatening to erupt into full-scale riot, the overseers of the poor did their best to alleviate the misery of those in their charge. Revolution was avoided but the price was financial as well as social and moral.

William Hale to Patrick Colquhoun, 21st October 1800
Quoted in English Historical Documents, Vol XI

. . . in the discharge of my parochial office I am frequently called upon to witness scenes of the most awful distress; to visit families who, to satisfy the cravings of hunger, have long ago been forced to part with their clothes and linen, and, almost expiring amidst the awful horrors of starvation, have scarcely a rag to cover their nakedness. An apothecary not far from me informing me a few weeks back of the dreadful situation of the poor, told me that in the course of his practice since last November he knows of above a hundred cases of children dying for want of food, and of about 40 grown-up people that had also fell [sic] victims to that awful calamity; . . .

Where people are for a time out of employ, or through sickness are not able to work, their situation is dreadful in the extreme. As an overseer I am frequently under the necessity of visiting such scenes of distress, and yet have not the means of giving them an adequate relief. I leave their dismal habitations with the bitter reflection that their *weekly* pittance which I had just given them, is not sufficient to purchase a competency of the single article of bread for *one day*. I am far from wishing to describe the situation of the lower class of people in Spitalfields to be worse than the poor of other parishes. To speak in general terms as to their employment &c &c they are not, and had we but a certain proportion of poor as in other parishes, we could give them a proportionable and suitable relief; but it is their number that ruins us, and which makes it totally impossible for us to give them that succour their distressed situation requires.

I was at our workhouse near the whole of yesterday. The number of our paupers in the house then was 412. It is considerably more than full. We are obliged to put them three and in some cases four in a bed. Our parochial expenses daily increase upon us, and our debt daily accumulates. The amount of debts that we owe to the mealman, butcher, &c without any present ability to pay is £1972–16–5½, and though we had made use of every means to abridge the expense, and observed the most strict economy in all the Departments, we had the additional mortification to find we were £396–17–2 worse than we were at Midsummer. Before we can now pay any tradesman a quarter's bill, we are four quarters in arrears with him, in consequence of which we in some instances begin to find it difficult to purchase the necessary articles of life without great disadvantage. . . . A great part of our poor rates are wrung from those families who, I am certain, are not able to pay. Many of them are summoned, who appeal to the Magistrate; some are excused half the sum, and others do not pay at all. Many that are respectable mechanics in this parish, and contributed to the relief of the poor, unable to bear up under the pressure of the times, have had their goods seized. Their poverty has descended into indigency, the pride of their independency is broke, and they become paupers of the parish.

Malthus on the Poor Laws

The escalation of the cost of maintaining the poor in their poverty attracted the attention of numerous contemporaries and some severe remedies were proposed.

T. R. Malthus, First Essay on Population 1798
Quoted in English Historical Documents, Vol XI

To remedy the frequent distresses of the common people, the poor Laws of England have been instituted; but it is to be feared, that though they may have alleviated a little the intensity of individual misfortune, they have spread the general evil over a much larger surface. It is a subject often started in conversation, and mentioned always as a matter of great surprise, that notwithstanding the immense sum that is annually collected for the poor in England, there is still so much distress among them. Some think that the money must be embezzled; others that the church-wardens and overseers consume the greater part of it in dinners. All agree that some how or other it must be very ill-managed. . . .

The poor-laws of England tend to depress the general condition of the poor in these two ways. Their first obvious tendency is to increase population without increasing the food for its support. A poor man may marry with little or no prospect of being able to support a family in independence. They may be said therefore in some measure to create the poor which they maintain; and as the provisions of the country must, in consequence of the increased population, be distributed to every man in smaller proportions, it is evident that the labour of those who are not supported by parish assistance, will purchase a smaller quantity of provisions than before and consequently, more of them must be driven to ask for support.

Secondly, the quantity of provisions consumed in workhouses upon a part of the society, that cannot in general be considered as the most valuable part, diminishes the shares that would otherwise belong to more industrious, and more worthy members; and thus in the same manner forces more to become dependent. If the poor in the workhouses were to live better than they now do, this new distribution of the money of society would tend more conspicuously to depress the condition of those out of the workhouses, by occasioning a rise in the price of provisions.

Fortunately for England, a spirit of independence still remains among the peasantry. The poor-laws are strongly calculated to eradicate this spirit. They have succeeded in part; but had they succeeded as completely as might have been expected, their pernicious tendency would not have been so long concealed.

Hard as it may appear in individual instances, dependent poverty ought to be held disgraceful. Such a stimulus seems to be absolutely necessary to promote the happiness of the great mass of mankind; and every general attempt to weaken this stimulus, however benevolent its apparent intention, will always defeat its own purpose. If men are induced to marry from a prospect of parish provision, with little or no chance of maintaining their families in independence, they are not only unjustly tempted to bring unhappiness and dependence upon themselves and children; but they are tempted, without knowing it, to injure all in the same class with themselves. A labourer who marries without being able to support a family, may in some respects be considered as an enemy to all his fellow-labourers.

... Were I to propose a palliative; and palliatives are all that the nature of the case will admit; it should be, in the first place, the total abolition of all the present parish-laws. This would at any rate give liberty and freedom of action to the peasantry of England, which they can hardly be said to possess at present. They would then be able to settle without interruption, wherever there was a prospect of a greater plenty of work, and a higher price for labour. ...

Tom Paine's Solution

DOCUMENT 175

From Thomas Paine, Rights of Man (1791), Part II, pp 227–8

I shall now conclude this plan with enumerating the several particulars, and then proceed to other matters:

The enumeration is as follows:

First—Abolition of two millions poor-rates.

Secondly—Provision for two hundred and fifty thousand poor families.

Thirdly—Education for one million and thirty thousand children.

Fourthly—Comfortable provision for one hundred and forty thousand aged persons.

Fifthly—Donation of twenty shillings each for fifty thousand births.

Sixthly—Donation of twenty shillings each for twenty thousand marriages

Seventhly—Allowances of twenty thousand pounds for the funeral expenses of persons travelling for work, and dying at a distance from their friends.

Eighthly—Employment at all times, for the casual poor in the cities of London and Westminster.

By the operation of this plan, the poor laws, those instruments of civil torture, will be superseded, and the wasteful expence of litigation prevented. The hearts of the humane will not be shocked by ragged and hungry children, and persons of seventy and eighty years of age, begging for bread. The dying poor will not be dragged from place to place to breathe their last, as a reprisal of parish upon parish. Widows will have a maintenance for their children, and not be carted away, on the death of their husbands, like culprits and criminals; and children will no longer be considered as encreasing the distresses of their parents. The haunts of the wretched will be known, because it will be to their advantage, and the number of petty crimes, the offspring of distress and poverty will be lessened. The poor, as well as the rich, will then be interested in the support of government, and the cause and apprehension of riots and tumults will cease.

The Effects of Depression

The seasonal demands of agriculture led to fluctuations in employment and income for rural labourers. Textile workers depended on the volatile fortunes of foreign markets.

DOCUMENT 176

Greville, Memoirs, 17th February 1832

A man came yesterday from Bethnal Green with an account of that district. They are all weavers, forming a sort of separate community; there they are born, there they live and labour, and there they die. They neither migrate nor change their occupation; they can do nothing else. They have increased in a ratio at variance with any principles of population, having nearly tripled in twenty years, from 22,000 to 62,000. They are for the most part out of employment, and can get none. 1,100 are crammed into the poor-house, five or six in a bed; 6,000 receive parochial relief. The parish is in debt; every day adds to the number of paupers and diminishes that of ratepayers. These are principally small shopkeepers, who are beggared by the rates. The district is in a complete state of insolvency and hopeless poverty, yet they multiply, and while the people look squalid and dejected, as if borne down by their wretchedness and destitution, the children thrive and are healthy. Government is ready to interpose with assistance, but what can Government do? We asked the man who came what could be done for them. He said 'employment', and employment is impossible.

The Burden of Taxes

Taxes, designed to raise revenue to pay off the vastly inflated National Debt, fell chiefly on those least able to bear them.

DOCUMENT 177

S.C. on Hand-Loom Weavers' Petitions (1834), pp 293 ff. The witness, R. M. Martin, was author of Taxation of the British Empire (1833) Quoted in E. P. Thompson, The Making of the English Working Class

No. 1. Tax on malt, £4. 11s. 3d. No. 2. On sugar, 17s. 4d. No. 3. Tea or coffee, £1 4s. No. 4. On soap, 13s. No 5. Housing, 12s. No. 6. On food,

£3. No. 7. On clothing, 10s. Total taxes on the labourer per annum, £11 7s. 7d. Taking a labourer's earnings at 1s. 6d. per diem, and computing his working 300 days in the year (which very many do), this income will be £22 10s.; thus it will be admitted that at the very least, 100 per cent, or half of his income is abstracted from him by taxation . . . for do what he will, eating, drinking, or sleeping, he is in some way or other taxed.

Technological redundancy was threatening increasing numbers of workers. The most tragic case is that of the hand-loom weavers, who numbered 250,000 in the 1830s, and were almost totally eliminated in the following two decades.

DOCUMENT 178

Porter, Progress of the Nation, p 126

In every country which is making any considerable progress in the arts of life, changes will from time to time occur in the sources of employment for particular classes of people, which must be felt as a hardship by individuals, although to the country at large they are productive of great and permanent good. The introduction of the power-loom, which has so vastly increased the productive force of the kingdom, has worked, and still is working injuriously to a numerous body of hand-loom weavers who cannot always find employment in other branches of industry without suffering great inconveniences and privations, and who are liable to be thrown wholly out of employment, or, at best, may be obliged to submit to a scale of wages inadequate to their wants.

Plight of the Weavers

The attitude of government remained one of fatalistic resignation.

DOCUMENT 179

Journals of the House of Commons and Hansard, passim; Reports of Hand-Loom Weavers' Commissioners (1840), Part III, p. 590
Quoted in E. P. Thompson, The Making of the English Working Class

The power of the Czar of Russia, it was reported, could not raise the wages of men so situate . . . all that remains, therefore, is to enlighten the handloom weavers as to their real situation, warn them to flee from the trade, and to beware of leading their children into it, as they would beware the commission of the most atrocious of crimes.

The Workhouse

The New Poor Law of 1834 was designed to give the 'invisible hand' a nudge. By denying poor relief except upon the harshest terms it was hoped to lubricate the labour market by forcing men to seek out work rather than to enter the poorhouse.

DOCUMENT 180

Report of the Royal Commission for Inquiring into the Administration and Practical Operation of the Poor Laws (1834), XXVII, p 146

By the workhouse system is meant having all relief through the workhouse, making this workhouse an uninviting place of wholesome restraint, preventing any of its inmates from going out or receiving visitors, without a written order to that effect from one of the overseers, disallowing beer and tobacco, and finding them work according to their ability: thus making the parish fund the last resource of a pauper, and rendering the person who administers the relief the hardest taskmaster and the worst paymaster that the idle and the dissolute can apply to.

The New Poor Law Denounced

The New Poor Law roused immediate antagonism, particularly in the North, where the problem was one of cyclical unemployment in manufacturing industry, not structural unemployment in agriculture. Agitation against the new workhouses turned eventually into agitation for sweeping political change and the implementation of the 'People's Charter'.

DOCUMENT 181

From G. R. Wythen Baxter, The Book of the Bastiles (1841), Introduction, pp iii–iv
Quoted in Cole and Filson, British Working Class Movements, Selected Documents 1789–1875

. . . the paramount reason for publishing the Book of the Bastiles was, the urgent necessity in the present alarming crisis—a crisis mainly attributable to the operation of such harsh, biting statutes as the New Poor-Law—of calling the attention of the upper and middle classes to the inhumanity, unchristianity, injustice, and political and social danger of the continued administration of the New Poor-Law Amendment-Act in England and Wales.

Had there been no lettre de cachet, the revolutionary Marseillaise would

174

never have been tuned in retribution, and Louis XVI would have died in his bed, and not on the block. Had there been no New Poor-Law, the name of Chartist would never have been heard; nor would Birmingham have been heated with fire and fury, or Newport have run red with the gore of Britons from the hills. . . .

In the North opposition to the workhouse enjoyed some success, even in the face of military occupation. In the rest of the country the severity of the new policy was untempered.

DOCUMENT 182

F. Engels, The Condition of the Working Class in England in 1844, pp 286–7

Since, however, the rich hold all the power, the proletarians must submit, if they will not good-temperedly perceive it for themselves, to have the law actually declare them superfluous. This has been done by the New Poor Law. The Old Poor Law which rested upon the Act of 1601 (the 43rd of Elizabeth), naively started from the notion that it is the duty of the parish to provide for the maintenance of the poor. Whoever had no work received relief, and the poor man regarded the parish as pledged to protect him from starvation. He demanded his weekly relief as his right, not as a favour, and this became, at last, too much for the bourgeoisie. In 1833, when the bourgeoisie had just come into power through the Reform Bill, and pauperism in the country districts had just reached its full development, the bourgeoisie began the reform of the Poor Law according to its own point of view. A commission was appointed, which investigated the administration of the Poor Laws, and revealed a multitude of abuses. It was discovered that the whole working-class in the country was pauperised and more or less dependent upon the rates, from which they received relief when wages were low; it was found that this system by which the unemployed were maintained, the ill-paid and the parents of large families relieved, fathers of illegitimate children required to pay alimony, and poverty, in general, recognised as needing protection, it was found that this system was ruining the nation, was—

'A check upon industry, a reward for improvident marriage, a stimulus to increased population, and a means of counterbalancing the effect of an increased population upon wages; a national provision for discouraging the honest and industrious, and protecting the lazy, vicious, and improvident; calculated to destroy the bonds of family life, hinder systematically the accumulation of capital, scatter that which is already accumulated, and ruin the taxpayers. Moreover, in the provision of aliment, it sets a premium upon illegitimate children.'

(Words of the Report of the Poor Law Commissioners (1833)). This description of the action of the Old Poor Law is certainly correct; relief fosters laziness and increase of 'surplus population'. Under present social conditions it is perfectly clear that the poor man is compelled to be an egotist, and when he can choose, living equally well in either case, he prefers doing nothing to working. But what follows therefrom? That our present social conditions are good for nothing, and not as the Malthusian Commissioners conclude, that poverty is a crime, and, as such, to be visited with heinous penalties which may serve as a warning to others.

But these wise Malthusians were so thoroughly convinced of the infallibility of their theory that they did not for one moment hesitate to cast the poor into the Procrustean bed of their economic notions and treat them with the most revolting cruelty. Convinced with Malthus and the rest of the adherents of free competition that it is best to let each one take care of himself, they would have preferred to abolish the Poor Laws altogether. Since, however, they had neither the courage nor the authority to do this, they proposed a Poor Law constructed as far as possible in harmony with the doctrine of Malthus, which is yet more barbarous than that of laissez-faire, because it interferes actively in cases in which the latter is passive. We have seen how Malthus characterises poverty or rather the want of employment, as a crime under the title 'Superfluity', and recommends for it punishment by starvation. The commissioners were not quite so barbarous; death outright by starvation was something too terrible even for a Poor Law Commissioner. 'Good,' said they, 'we grant you poor a right to exist, but only to exist; the right to multiply you have not, nor the right to exist as befits human beings. You are a pest, and if we cannot get rid of you as we do of other pests, you shall feel, at least, that you are a pest, and you shall at least be held in check, kept from bringing into the world other "surplus", either directly or through inducing in others laziness and want of employment. Live you shall, but live as an awful warning to all those who might have inducements to become "superfluous".'

They accordingly brought in the New Poor Law, which was passed by Parliament in 1834, and continues in force down to the present day. All relief in money and provisions was abolished; the only relief allowed was admission to the workhouses immediately built. The regulations for these workhouses, or, as the people call them, Poor Law Bastilles, is such as to frighten away every one who has the slightest prospect of life without this form of public charity. To make sure that relief be applied for only in the most extreme cases and after every other effort had failed, the workhouse has been made the most repulsive residence which the refined ingenuity of a Malthusian can invent. The food is worse than that of the most ill-paid working-man while employed, and the work harder, or they might prefer the workhouse to their wretched existence outside. Meat, especially fresh meat, is rarely furnished, chiefly potatoes, the worst possible bread and oat-meal porridge, little or no beer. The food of criminal prisoners is better, as a rule, so that

176

the paupers frequently commit some offence for the purpose of getting into jail. For the workhouse is a jail too; he who does not finish his task gets nothing to eat; he who wishes to go out must ask permission, which is granted or not, according to his behaviour or the inspector's whim, tobacco is forbidden, also the receipt of gifts from relatives or friends outside the house; the paupers wear a workhouse uniform, and are handed over, helpless and without redress, to the caprice of the inspectors. To prevent their labour from competing with that of outside concerns, they are set to rather useless tasks. The men break stones, 'as much as a strong man can accomplish with effort in a day;' the women, children, and aged men pick oakum, for I know not what insignificant use. To prevent the 'superfluous' from multiplying, and 'demoralised' parents from influencing their children, families are broken up, the husband is placed in one wing, the wife in another, the children in a third, and they are permitted to see one another only at stated times after long intervals, and then only when they have, in the opinion of the officials, behaved well. And in order to shut off the external world from contamination by pauperism within these bastilles, the inmates are permitted to receive visits only with the consent of the officials, and in the reception-rooms; to communicate in general with the world outside only by leave and under supervision.

Emigration, Solution to Poverty

For the young, the strong, the unattached and the intelligent emigration offered the best way out of a buyer's labour market. But those who were most exploited were too poor, too beaten to take advantage of the opportunity which North America offered them.

DOCUMENT 183

Cobden to W. C. Hunt, 1836
Quoted in K. Dawsen and P. Wall, Industry and Society in the 19th Century, Vol 2, Factory Reform.

Am I told that the industrious classes of Lancashire are incapable of protecting themselves from oppression unless by the shield of the legislature? I am loath to believe it. Nay, as I am opposed to the plan of legislating upon such a subject, I am bound to suggest another remedy. I would, then, advise the working classes to make themselves free of the labour market of the world, and this they can do by accumulating twenty pounds each, which will give them the command of the only market in which labour is at a higher rate than in England—I mean that of the United States. If every working man would save this sum, he might be as independent of his employer as the latter, with his great capital, is of his workman. Were this universal, we should hear no more of the tyranny of the employers.

177

Emigration to America 1830

The Atlantic trade in timber and cotton supported enough shipping to make a reciprocal trade in immigrants worth while. By the middle years of the century one could cross to America for three or four pounds but the passage was a test of endurance.

DOCUMENT 184

William Cobbett, Rural Rides, II, 19th April 1830

The way to New York is now as well known and as little expensive as from old York to London. First the Sussex parishes sent their paupers; they invited over others that were not paupers; they invited over people of some property; then persons of greater property; now substantial farmers are going; men of considerable fortune will follow. It is the letters written across the Atlantic that do the business. Men of fortune will soon discover that, to secure to their families their fortunes, and to take these out of the grasp of the inexorable tax-gatherer, they must get away. Every one that goes will take twenty after him; and thus it will go on. There can be no interruption but *war*: and war the Thing dares not have. As to France or the Netherlands, or any part of that hell called Germany, Englishmen can never settle there. The United States form another England without its unbearable taxes, its insolent game laws, its intolerable dead-weight, and its treadmills.

Emigration to America 1850

The Irish famine of 1845–6 prompted the emigration of more than a million persons and the population of Ireland continued to decline until the 1920s.

DOCUMENT 185

Illustrated London News, 1850

The great tide of Emigration flows steadily westward. The principal emigrants are Irish peasants and labourers. It is calculated that at least four out of every five persons who leave the shores of the old country to try their fortunes in the new, are Irish. Since the fatal years of the potato famine and the cholera, the annual numbers of emigrants have become so great as to suggest the idea, and almost justify the belief, of a gradual depopulation of Ireland. The colonies of Great Britain offer powerful attractions to the great bulk of the English and Scottish emigrants who forsake their native land to make homes in the wilderness. But the Irish emigration flows with full force upon the United States. Though many of the Irish emigrants are, doubtless, persons of small means, the great bulk appear to be people of the most destitute class, who go to join their friends and relatives, previously established in America.

The emigration of the present year (1850) bids fair to exceed even the unprecedentedly large emigration of 1849. This human stream flows principally through the ports of London and Liverpool; as there is but little direct emigration from Scotland or Ireland. In the year 1849, out of the total number of 299,498 emigrants, more than one half left from the port of Liverpool. We learn from a statement in a Liverpool newspaper, that in the months of January, February and March, and April of the present year, the total emigration was 50,683 persons; and as these four months include two of the least busy months of the year, it is probable that the numbers during the months of May, June and July, and August, the full emigrational season, will be much more considerable, and that the emigration for the year will exceed that for 1849.

It would appear that very few out of the vast army of Irish and other emigrants that proceed to the United States or the British Colonies, go out as mere adventurers, without some knowledge of the country, or their chances of doing well, when they get there. The sums received by them before they leave this country are sufficient proof that they have prosperous friends upon the other side; and it is to be presumed that the friends who send them the money, do not avoid sending them advice, and giving them full information, to the best of their means, as to their movements upon arrival.

No passenger-ship is allowed to proceed until a medical practitioner appointed by the emigration office of the port shall have inspected the medicine chest and passengers, and certified that the medicines etc. are sufficient, and the passengers are free from contagious disease.

There are usually a large number of spectators at the dock-gates to witness the final departure of the noble ship, with its large freight of human beings. It is an interesting and impressive sight, and the most callous and indifferent can scarcely fail, at such a moment, to form cordial wishes for the pleasant voyage and safe arrival of the emigrants, and for their future prosperity in their new home. As the ship is towed, hats are raised, handkerchiefs are waved, and a loud and long-continued shout of farewell is raised from the shore, and cordially responded to from the ship. May all prosperity attend her living freight!

The Reality of Progress

Problems of Evidence

Despite the wide public discussion which the 'Condition of England' question provoked in the 1830s and 1840s, there is an embarrassing lack of accurate statistical material relating to this period.

DOCUMENT 186

McCulloch (ed.), A Statistical Account of the British Empire (1839),
Vol II, pp. 507–8
Quoted in Coats, 'The Classical Economists and the Labourer in Land',
'Labour and Population in the Industrial Revolution', ed. Jones & Mingay

There is no subject about which so many contradictory assertions are made, by those pretending to be acquainted with it, as the state of the middle and lower classes in all parts of the country. We, in fact, *Have no real knowledge of the matter.* There are no authentic accounts of the qualities and current prices of articles in any great market, the rent of houses and lodgings, the rate of wages in proportion to the work done, and a variety of other particulars, indispensable to be known before anyone can pretend to estimate the condition of the bulk of the people, or to compare their state at one period with their state at another. . . . Ministers are quite as much in the dark as to these matters as other people. The Secretary for the Home Department is about as well informed respecting the demand for labour, wages, diet, dress and other accommodations of the people of Canton and Manilla, as of those of Manchester and Paisley.

Exciseable goods like tea and coffee have left their mark in official records but information on major items of expenditure, like rent or fuel, is fragmentary.

DOCUMENT 187

G. R. Porter, Progress of the Nation, p 537

There are no means provided by which the consumption of the prime necessaries of life in this country can be traced at different periods. It is only with respect to those few articles of native production which have been subjected to the payment of duties that any provision has ever been made for ascertaining their quantity; and as the chief articles of food and clothing, when of such production have never been directly taxed in England, we have always been ignorant in this respect regarding the quantities produced.

The want of this information has been found greatly inconvenient, both by statesmen and by writers on subjects of social economy, the latter of whom have frequently had recourse to the expedient of computations founded on insufficient data, and which have therefore given an unsatisfactory character to their writings.

The Price of Economic Growth

The desire to lay up riches in this world prompted entrepreneurs to reinvest their profits and redouble their efforts when their ventures were blessed with success. Certain sections of society seem to have been afflicted with a 'growthmania' which made them lose sight of the larger purposes of life.

DOCUMENT 188

Karl Marx (1867), Das Kapital, Vol I, p 652

Accumulate, accumulate! That is Moses and the prophets! . . . Accumulation for accumulation's sake, production for production's sake. . . .

John Stuart Mill, a noted economist and political thinker, believed that material progress was being purchased at too great a social cost.

DOCUMENT 189

J. S. Mill, Principles of Political Economy, p 748

I cannot . . . regard the stationary state of capital and wealth with the un-affected aversion so generally manifested towards it by political economists of the old school. I am inclined to believe that it would be, on the whole, a very considerable improvement on our present condition. I confess that I am not charmed with the ideal of life held out by those who think that the normal state of human beings is that of struggling to get on; the trampling, crushing, elbowing, and treading on each other's heels, which form the existing type of social life, are the most desirable lot of human kind, or anything but the most disagreeable symptoms of one of the phases of industrial progress.

Carlyle felt that, far from representing the triumph of the individual spirit, the industrial age marked its demise.

DOCUMENT 190

T. Carlyle, Signs of the Times (1829)
Quoted in Raymond Williams, Culture and Society, p 86

Not the external and physical alone is now managed by machinery but the internal and spiritual also . . . The same habit regulates not our modes of action alone, but our modes of thought and feeling. Men are grown mechanical in head and heart, as well as in hand. They have lost faith in individual endeavours, and in natural force, of any kind. Not for internal perfection, but for external combinations and arrangements for institutions, constitutions, for Mechanism of one sort or another, do they hope and struggle.

The explosion of social and individual wealth which industrialisation precipitated was not marked by any notable flowering of culture. Education was paralysed by the differences of religious factions and the English middle classes were becoming renowned for their Philistinism.

DOCUMENT 191

S. Laing, Notes of A Traveller on the Social and Political State of France,
Prussia, Switzerland, Italy and other parts of Europe (1842) (1854 ed.),
p 275

In proportion to the wealth of the country, how few in Great Britain are the buildings of any note . . . how little is the absorption of capital in museums, pictures, gems, curiosities, palaces, theatres or other unreproductive objects!

Despite man's increasing mastery over the forces of nature, fluctuations in international trade or a run of bad harvests could still paralyse the productive efforts of the most advanced society in the known world.

DOCUMENT 192

Greville, Memoirs, 2nd November 1842

Lord Wharncliffe and Kay Shuttleworth, who are both come from the north, have given me an account of the state of the country and of the people which is perfectly appalling. There is an immense and continually increasing population, deep distress and privation, no adequate demand for labour, no demand for anything, no confidence, but a universal alarm, disquietude, and discontent. Nobody can sell anything. Somebody said, speaking of some part of Yorkshire, 'This is certainly the happiest country in the world, for *nobody wants anything.*' Kay says that nobody can conceive the state of demoralisation of the people, of the masses, and that the only thing which restrains them from acts of violence against property is a sort of instinctive consciousness that, bad as things are, their own existence depends upon the security of property *in the long run.* It is in these parts that the worst symptoms are apparent, but there are indications of the same kind more or less all over the country, and certainly I have never seen, in the course of my life, so serious a state of things as that which now stares us in the face; and this, after thirty years of uninterrupted peace, and the most ample scope afforded for the development of all our resources, when we have been altering, amending, and improving, wherever we could find anything to work upon, and being, according to our own ideas, not only the most free and powerful, but the most moral and the wisest people in the world. One remarkable feature in the present condition of affairs is that nobody can account for it, and nobody pretends to be able to point out any remedy; for those who clamour for the repeal of the Corn Laws, at least those who know anything of the matter, do not really believe that repeal would supply a cure for our distempers. It is certainly a very dismal matter for reflection, and well worthy the consideration of the profoundest political philosophers, that the possession of such a Constitution, all our wealth, industry, ingenuity, peace, and that superiority in wisdom and virtue which we so confidently claim, are not sufficient to prevent the existence of a huge mountain of human misery, of one stratum in society in the most deplorable state, both moral and physical, to which mankind can be reduced, and that all our advantages do not secure us against the occurrence of evils and mischiefs so great as to threaten a mighty social and political convulsion.

The Reality of Progress

In the year of the Great Exhibition Englishmen felt they had some cause for self-congratulation.

DOCUMENT 193

The Economist, 1851
Quoted in E. Royston Pike, Human Documents of the Victorian Golden Age

Perhaps the best way of realizing . . . the actual progress of the last half-century would be to fancy ourselves suddenly transferred to the year 1800, with all our habits, expectations, requirements, and standard of living formed upon the luxuries and appliances collected round us in 1850.

In the first year of the century we should find ourselves eating bread at
1s. 10½d. the quartern loaf, and those who could not afford this price driven
to short commons, to entire abstinence, or to some miserable substitute.
We should find ourselves grumbling at heavy taxes laid on nearly all the
necessaries and luxuries of life—even upon salt; blaspheming at the high
price of coffee, tea and sugar, which confined these articles, in any adequate
abundance, to the rich and easy classes of society; paying fourfold for our
linen shirts, threefold for our flannel petticoats, and above fivefold for our
cotton handkerchiefs and stockings; receiving our newspapers seldom . . .
and some days after date; receiving our Edinburgh letters in London a week
after they were written, and paying thirteen pence-halfpenny for them when
delivered; exchanging the instantaneous telegraph for the slow and costly
express by chaise and pair; travelling with soreness and fatigue by the 'old
heavy' (coach) at the rate of seven miles an hour, instead of by the Great
Western (railway) at fifty; and relapsing from the blaze of light which gas
now pours along our streets, into a perilous and uncomfortable darkness
made visible by a few wretched oil lamps scattered at distant intervals.

. . . Finally, the *people* in those days were little thought of, where they
are now the main topic of discourse and statesmanship; steamboats were
unknown, and a voyage to America occupied eight weeks instead of ten
days; and while in 1850, a population of nearly 30,000,000 paid £50,000,000
taxes, in 1801 a population of 15,000,000 paid no less than £63,000,000.

Consumption

DOCUMENT 194

G. R. Porter, Progress of the Nation, p 522

. . . It has been argued, by high authorities, that there is under all circumstances a tendency in population to press upon the means of subsistence.
If, however, we look back to the condition of the mass of the people as it
existed in this country, even so recently as the beginning of the present
century, and then look around us at the indications of greater comfort and
respectability that meet us on every side, it is hardly possible to doubt
that here, in England at least, the elements of social improvement have been
successfully at work, and that they have been and are producing an increased
amount of comfort to the great bulk of the people. This improvement is
by no means confined to those who are called, by a somewhat arbitrary
distinction, the working classes, but is enjoyed in some degree or other by
tradesmen, shopkeepers, farmers,—in short, by every class of men whose
personal and family comforts admitted of material increase. Higher in the
scale of society, the same cause has been productive of increase of luxury,
of increased encouragement to science, literature, and the fine arts, and of
additions to the elegancies of life, the indulgence in which has acted upon the

condition of the less-favoured classes directly by means of the additional employment it has caused, and indirectly also by reason of the general refinement in manners which has thus been brought about.

The Great Exhibition displayed Britain's productive power to the world as the whole nation symbolised the progress towards which the rest of mankind might struggle.

DOCUMENT 195

As quoted in Theodore Martin, Life of the Prince Consort

On the evening of May 1st, 1851, the Queen recorded in her diary:

The great event has taken place—a complete and beautiful triumph—a glorious and touching sight, one which I shall ever be proud of for my beloved Albert and my country. . . .

The Park presented a wonderful spectacle, crowds streaming through it, carriages and troops passing, quite like the Coronation day, and for me the same anxiety—no, much greater anxiety on account of my beloved Albert. The day was bright and all bustle and excitement. . . . The Green Park and Hyde Park were one densely crowded mass of human beings, in the highest good humour and most enthusiastic. I never saw Hyde Park look as it did—as far as the eye could reach. A little rain fell just as we started; but before we came near the Crystal Palace the sun shone and gleamed upon the gigantic edifice, upon which the flags of all Nations were floating. We drove up Rotten Row and got out at the entrance on that side.

The glimpse of the transept through the iron gates, the waving palms, flowers, statues, myriads of people filling the galleries and seats around, with the flourish of trumpets as we entered, gave us a sensation which I can never forget, and I felt much moved. . . . In a few seconds we proceeded, Albert leading me, having Vicky at his hand, and Bertie holding mine. The sight as we came to the middle . . . with the beautiful Crystal fountain . . . so vast, so glorious, so touching. One felt—as so many did whom I have since spoken to—filled with devotion—more so than by any service I have ever heard. The tremendous cheers, the joy expressed in every face, the immensity of the building, the mixture of palms, flowers, trees, statues, fountains—the organ (with 200 instruments and 600 voices, which sounded like nothing), and my beloved husband the author of this 'Peace Festival', which united the industry of all nations of the earth—all this was moving indeed, and it was and is a day to live for ever. . . .

Index